THE FROZEN FOUNTAIN

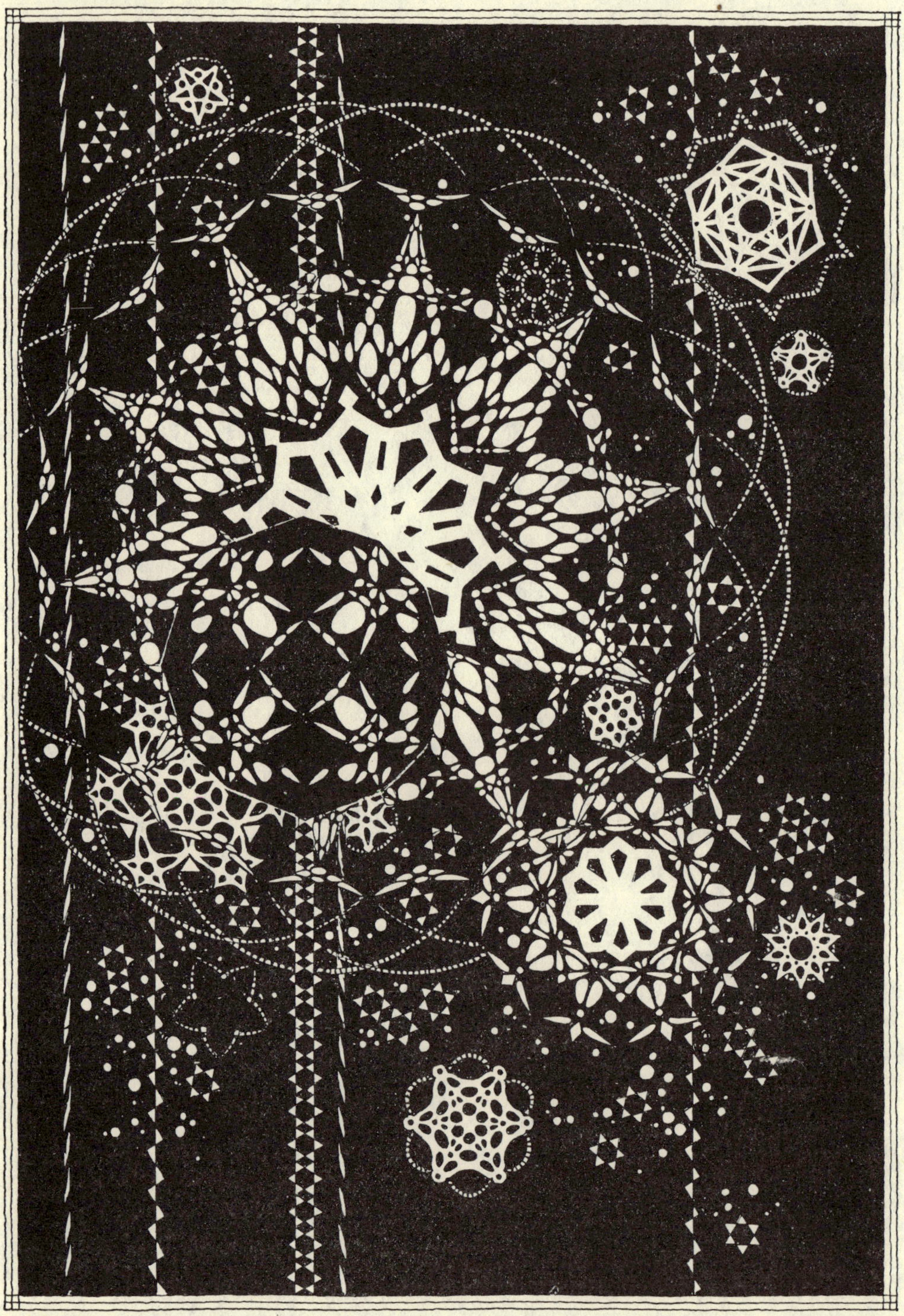

The FROZEN FOUNTAIN

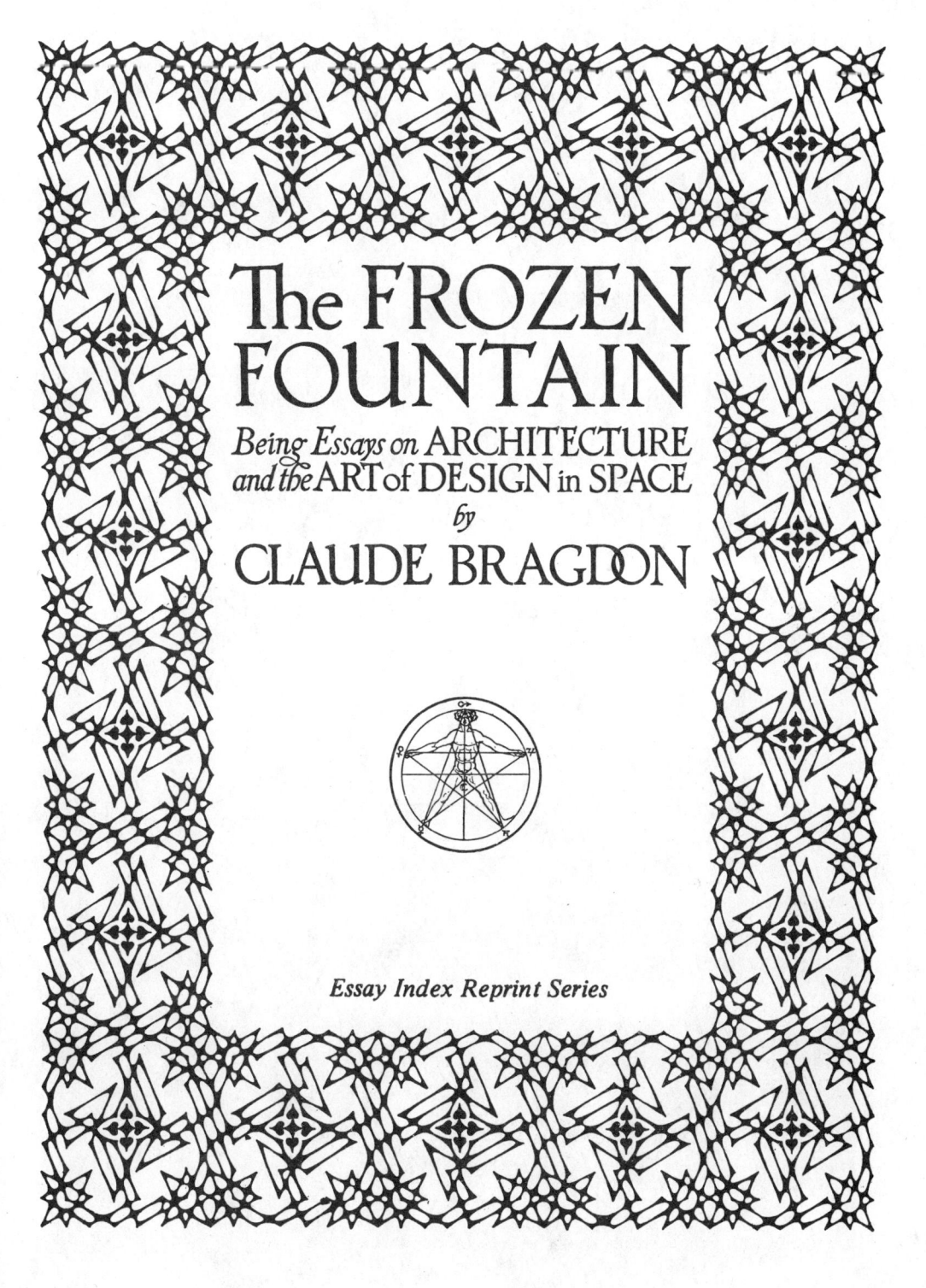

Being Essays on ARCHITECTURE
and the ART *of* DESIGN *in* SPACE
by
CLAUDE BRAGDON

Essay Index Reprint Series

BOOKS FOR LIBRARIES PRESS
FREEPORT, NEW YORK

Copyright © 1924, 1926, 1928, 1931, 1932 by Claude Bragdon

Reprinted 1970 by arrangement with Alfred A. Knopf, Inc.

INTERNATIONAL STANDARD BOOK NUMBER:
0-8369-1784-7

LIBRARY OF CONGRESS CATALOG CARD NUMBER:
75-127589

PRINTED IN THE UNITED STATES OF AMERICA

For permission to reprint some of the material included in this book thanks are due to *The Architectural Record, The Yale University Press, Architecture, Pencil Points, The American Mercury,* and *The Outlook and Independent.*

CONTENTS

	Introduction	1
I	FOUNDATION STONES	4
II	THE FROZEN FOUNTAIN	8
III	RETROSPECT	19
IV	THE SKYSCRAPER	25
V	REGULATING LINES	36
VI	ISOMETRIC PERSPECTIVE	58
VII	ORNAMENT	70
VIII	TO BE SKIPPED BY THE CASUAL READER	102
IX	COLOR	116

THE FROZEN FOUNTAIN

SINBAD SUMMONED FROM THE INK-BOTTLE, AND SENT FORTH ON HIS VOYAGE

INTRODUCTION

THIS book is addressed to everyone interested in the fine arts, to designers in all fields, and particularly to architects, architectural students, and draughtsmen. It constitutes the final distillation of many years of thought and experimentation along unusual lines. Naturally, I am desirous that it shall be read and pondered, but according to the habit of the day there are many who will only skim it and look at the pictures. Realizing this, I have tried to cram these as full of meaning and interest as possible, making them self-explanatory and provocative. To this end I have had recourse to a most ancient device, one used by Dürer and Hogarth. It consists in many different presentations of the same symbolical character in situations and surroundings which are themselves symbolical — as in *The Dance of Death,* and *The Rake's Progress.*

To my fictional protagonist I have given the name of Sinbad, not alone for the reason that this Arabian voyager had many strange adventures in strange lands, and might have unchronicled others, but the name itself seemed appropriate because — well, aren't we all? I mean, of course, bad sinners. It is a synonym for Everyman, which is what I wanted — the reader, the author, the candlestick-maker: that is, more specifically, the artist. This is a sort of *Pilgrim's Progress*. John Bunyan's masterpiece is a serious book, but so entertaining that my mother used to read it aloud to me when I was a child. *This* is a serious book, but with Sinbad's help I have tried to make it amusing. The American Spirit, as Kipling says, is "stirred, like a child, by little things," and I have sought to honor this truth by a due observance.

The book deals largely with matters about which I have already written, and sometimes it even repeats, in a different form of words, for the benefit of the uninitiated reader, things which I have said elsewhere; but for this I offer no apology. Every author, however wide his interests or various his gifts, can write but one book — the book of *himself;* and because life perpetually unfolds, he writes it in installments. Now a serial should be accompanied by a synopsis of the antecedent chapters to make it comprehensible to the reader who comes upon the story for the first time. This is the only extenuation I have to offer for the echoes from my other books which may be found herein. Aimed to relieve the reader of the necessity of referring to those other books, these repetitions perform the office of the sandwich which saves one, on a journey, the trouble of going back to the inn.

I desire here to make acknowledgment of my indebtedness to the following books and authors:

Dynamic Symmetry: The Greek Vase, by Jay Hambidge (Yale University Press, New Haven, Conn.; 1902).
Proportional Form, by Samuel Colman and C. Arthur Coan (G. P. Putnam's Sons, New York and London; 1920).
Magic Squares and Cubes, by W. S. Andrews (The Open Court Publishing Company, Chicago; 1908).
Geometry of Four Dimensions, by Henry Parker Manning (The Macmillan Company, New York; 1914).
Traité élémentaire de géométrie à quatre dimensions, by E. Jouffret

INTRODUCTION

(Librairie du Bureau des Longitudes, de l'École Polytechnique, Paris, France).

Le Nombre d'or: Les Rhythmes, by Matila C. Ghyka (Librairie Gallimard, 43 Rue de Beaune, Paris, France).

SINBAD FINDS THE FOUNDATION STONES OF THE TEMPLE OF ARCHITECTURE

I
FOUNDATION STONES

THE LITERATURE of architecture is concerned almost exclusively with the history of the development of this or that style and the description and analysis of famous buildings. Of the fundamental principles upon which the architectural art is founded, few books have anything to say. But without this sort of elementary knowledge the architectural designer lacks criteria for intelligent self-criticism, misses the path of true creativeness, and is likely to commit the most atrocious blunders without being in the least aware.

However often I may appear to wander into this or that by-path, or fix my eyes too myopically on the here and now, my one controlling purpose is to attempt to supply — by direct statement, by implication, by illustration — the above mentioned lack, namely: criteria for the judgment of any work of architectural art belonging to the past; generic principles for the guidance of those who are working in this field at the present time and of those whose part it will be to determine the architecture of the time to come.

Reduced to text-book form, without amplification or illustration, these first principles may be stated thus:

Architecture is the art of *significant building*.

The dictionary definition of the word *significant* is: "having a meaning, expressive, suggestive, with pregnant or secret sense; not insignificant or negligible."

When it is added, therefore, that architecture is *dramatization,* it is only repeating the original statement in a different form of words. For to dramatize is to *make* significant, to bring out what is essential by suppression of the inessential; to render pregnant — to *eloquently express.*

But to express *what,* exactly?

First of all, the *idea* which is the *raison d'être* of every work of architectural art, without which it could no more exist than a sentence could exist without a thought. So far as possible a building should publish to the beholder the purpose which it subserves — what it is *for,* what it is *about,* why it is *as* it is and not otherwise. The human virtues of truthfulness and sincerity are architectural virtues too: a prison ought to look like a prison, and a church ought to look like a church. A steel-framed building should not be given the appearance of one of solid masonry; terra-cotta and cement should not be made to imitate stone; nor shingles, Spanish tile. By the terms of our definition these and similar practices stand condemned.

Expressed in a form of words made familiar by Louis Sullivan, the form should never belie the function, but should follow and express it, and the function should determine the form, as in the case of natural organisms. This amounts to saying that a work of architecture should be *organic, functional.*

To recapitulate: Architecture is pre-eminently the art of *significant form in space* — forms significant of their function: *dramatic,* by reason of their eloquence and expressiveness; *organic* by reason of their mutual interrelations and their adaptation of means to ends.

If every architectural designer would write these three words: SIGNIFICANT, DRAMATIC, ORGANIC, on the mirror before which he shaves each morning, there would be less insignificant, undramatic, inorganic architecture produced.

But this is not all: I have reserved until the last the thing which is the most important, as it is the most difficult to describe, belonging as it does to the higher dimension of consciousness. Forced to name it in a single word which could be understood by everyone, I should have to call it the *æsthetic* quality, which is more than a blend of the other three, however inextricably mixed up with them — æsthetic not in the narrow meaning of the term, " in accordance with good taste," but in the broader, deeper sense of *beautifulness.* To the intuitive-minded I dare speak its true name, which is *love,* ecstasy, without the operation of which in one form or another the highest beauty is impossible.

This is a spiritual essence, and as such, like the digit placed before three ciphers, it gives the other three essentials their value, for without it they are, from one point of view, *nothing.* It is by reason of love manifesting as beautifulness that a work of engineering becomes a work of architectural art. This quality of love our architecture conspicuously lacks. Compared with the cathedrals of Chartres, Amiens, and Paris, not enough love has gone into the making of our " cathedrals of commerce " — not enough prayer, not enough praise, not enough sacrifice; which is only another way of saying that in them the idea of profit triumphs over the idea of perfection. Caressed by sunlight, embraced by mist, they are sometimes made beautiful in their own despite — for love can perform that miracle — but they do not impress by reason of any beauty beyond the merely necessitous. Economy and efficiency are not, after all, everything, so to *significant, dramatic, organic,* let us add *ecstatic,* with this for an overword: " *Wake up and dream.*"

All this is simple, self-evident truth, and sound architectural doctrine; but it does not tell the whole story nor account for all the facts. For architecture is always and inevitably the handwriting on space of the soul of a people or of a period, and if that soul be frivolous, bombastic, mendacious, the very falsity of the architecture will constitute its essential truth — truth to the thing it stands for and represents. Moreover, such architecture may be justified on grounds other than those outlined; may even possess a beauty all its own.

For example, the architecture of the Renaissance when it became overripe — the Baroque — is, after all, "significant, dramatic, organic, ecstatic" after its own kind; gets to heaven, so to speak, in its own way, — and should not be dismissed as negligible because it lacks the austere sublimity of the Egyptian, the purity and logic of the Greek, the structural veracity of the Gothic. So while keeping to the straight but not narrow path traced in the beginning of this chapter, it should be recognized that there is more than one road to architectural salvation, that "some things can be done as well as others," and that the problem of "honesty" is not so simple as it may at first appear.

Mere honesty, though a basic architectural virtue, is not all-sufficing: a factory or a grain-elevator built on strictly utilitarian lines is honest, but this does not constitute it a work of architectural art. Engineering is no more all that there is to architecture than literateness is all that there is to literature; engineering is the root but not the flower. Architecture is as much beyond mere rational and economical *building* as Carlyle's *French Revolution* is beyond the artless babble of the chronicler:

> Beauty of a richer vein,
> Graces of a subtler strain

must now become the object of our quest.

What is this beauty and what are these graces? Where shall they be sought and how acquired? To answer these questions it is necessary to plunge deeper, and in so doing seem to digress.

SINBAD, FROM THE ROOF OF THE MEGOPOLIS, VIEWS THE CITY OF FROZEN FOUNTAINS

II

THE FROZEN FOUNTAIN

A WORK of art must portray not only a world-aspect, but *the world-order:* through and by means of the concrete and particular it should suggest the abstract and the generic — it must be not only *typical,* but *archetypal.* Truth to *fact* is not enough; truth to *life* is what is required; whatever story it may chance to tell, a work of art must also tell the story of creation.

Nature herself gives us the hint of how this can be done. A snowflake, for example, no matter how it may differ from every other snowflake, is in its double tetrahedral form and spine-like structure, revealatory of the nature of water-crystallization. The unique form is at the same time a formula of all possible snowflake forms.

Applying this principle to architecture, a building over and above revealing its character and function, should tell something of the nature of gravitation, suspension, tension; of the properties of form, color, light, and the *uniqueness* of materials — that concrete is cast in forms, that terra-cotta is molded and fired, that wood is sawn and planed, stone chiseled and marble polished in order that its maximum of beauty may appear. This is almost automatically accomplished by following the line of least resistance, by letting the material itself dictate its treatment — by *withworking,* to coin a word to fit the case.

These are matters of *right dramatization* of which nature is the great exemplar — nature, which tirelessly tells the story of creation to our unseeing eyes. It is significant in this connection that our two pioneer "functionalists," Louis Sullivan and his pupil Frank Lloyd Wright, were lovers and students of nature. In Sullivan's *The Autobiography of an Idea* a passionate feeling for nature is revealed. " I love nature ardently," he wrote me in a letter, and Wright once remarked while we were walking together in the woods, " I don't see how a man can be a good architect unless he lives near to nature." It is to their love of nature that I attribute the *naturalness* of their mental processes, their escape from that atrophy of the creative faculty which so often overcomes the schoolmen — students, not of nature, but of *art*. Sullivan, to be sure, was a Beaux Arts man, but he specifically states that the school did not give him his *start:* " My real start [he says in the *Autobiography*] was made when, as a very young child, living much out of doors, I received impressions from the shifting aspects of nature so deep, so penetrating, that they have persisted to this day."

Now to study nature does not mean to make charming little watercolors of natural objects. Harvey Ellis' aphorism, " One should go sketching with one's hands in one's pockets," indicates the more rewarding procedure: the study of nature, not in order to paint her portrait, but to pluck out the heart of her mystery — to discover, that is, the *law* according to which she works.

For " nature is the same in all her parts " : like an air with variations her visible music consists always and only in innumerable elaborations on one basic theme, and it is only the vast variety in form, color, material, in spatial magnitude and temporal duration which prevents us from perceiving this inner identity, in the same way that it is the dramatic skill and versatility of an " impersonator " in the matter of facial expression, intonation, gesture, which create the illusion of many different persons instead of always the same one.

What is this unit-form of nature, the archetype of all visible images?

What formula most perfectly expresses our sense of the life-process? Is it not an ascension and a declension — in brief, a fountain: a welling up of a force from some mysterious source, a faltering of the initial impulse by reason of some counter-aspect of that force, a subsidence, a *return* all imaged in the upward rush and downward fall of the waters of a fountain, a skyrocket, a stone flung from the hand into the air?

This of course tells us nothing of life's *meaning;* it is merely a symbol of the life-process. From nature we shall never learn life's meaning, for nature is all pictures and no text, and its images tell us only as much as we ourselves are able to read into them.

The idea once grasped that *life is a fountain,* we see always and everywhere fountains, fountains! — the sun itself, the up-drawn waters and the descending rain, the elm, the willow, the heart, the phallus, and the mammary gland. But what has all this to do with architecture, the reader may ask.

Everything! For if life is indeed a fountain — a *struggle upward* — and nature a symbolization of that struggle, a work of architecture must be that too: a presentation, in terms of ponderable beauty, of the interplay and adjustment of contradictory forces. What happens in a fountain and in its every drop happens also in a building and in all its parts, where stress and strain, compression and tension, thrust and counter-thrust are ceaselessly operative.

Accordingly it is the business of the architect to dramatize not only a building's purpose and function, but also the interplay of forces going on within it, and in so doing he will be dramatizing life itself. What constitutes a thing a work of art is this suggestion of the universal through and by means of the particular. The play of *Hamlet,* for example, is not only *the* life of *a* man, but *the life of man* — Everyman's struggle with his own self-elements, the enemies of his own household. In architecture these enemies, which are at the same time progenitors and friends, are *the forces of nature* — the scalding sun, the lashing wind, the disruptive frost, the insinuating rain: agents all in that apotheosis whereby, in the hands of a true dramatist, a work of engineering becomes a work of architectural art.

That architecture contains these deeper meanings, and that their showing-forth is a conditioning factor of architectural form is no new idea: Irving K. Pond's admirable book, *The Meaning of Architecture,* is an amplification of this conception of a building as a fountain: a resistance and a succumbing. It is an idea of such universality and truth that it cannot but augment the creative power of the architect who is alive to all its implications. It is a *usable* idea, fertile in ways I shall endeavor to make plain.

SINBAD SEES IN THE ADVANCING AND THE RETREATING WAVE AN EPITOME OF THE LIFE-PROCESS

A building a fountain: how clarifying a point of view! I have only to look out of my window at those upthrust acres of steel, brick, and concrete which hide the river, laten the sunrise, shadow the streets, and diminish the sky to see all in this aspect. The needle-pointed *flèche* of the Chrysler tower catches the sunlight like a fountain's highest expiring jet. The set-backs of the broad and massive lofts and industrials appear now in the semblance of cascades descending in successive stages from the summits to which they have been upthrust. The white vertical masses of the Waldorf-Astoria, topped with silver, seem a plexus of upward rushing, upward gushing fountains, most powerful and therefore highest at the center, descending by ordered stages to the broad Park Avenue river. I have but to sit, as I sometimes do, in the dim, quiet nave of St. Thomas' church in the near-by Fifth Avenue and fix my vision on its aligned piers of stone, expanding, fan-wise, into the groined vaulting, to see them as a succession of water-jets, fixed into immobility — time frozen into eternity. I have but to remember the dome and flanking minarets of Santa Sophia and of the Taj Mahal, Giotto's straight square bell-tower beside Brunelleschi's gigantic bubble, the obelisk of Thebes, the shrine of Vishnu at Khajuraho, the diminishing masses of which take on the contours of falling water, to see them all as frozen fountains thrust upward by the same mysterious energy which arises moment by moment in myself. For the very power whereby I perceive these things is the same power whereby they were themselves conceived — the power of the life-force, *one,* though infinitely differentiated and subdivided, as the water in a reservoir when hurled aloft is split up into pearly drops and crystal ribbons, like souls which, issuing from the Unconscious, trace each a shining parabola in space-time and subside again into the reservoir of life.

So let the architect say to himself not only, I shall build enclosures for the shelter and trafficking of human beings, but also, I shall create frozen fountains, with the vigor of geysers and the placidity of waters stilled at even. Such resolve and such endeavor will constitute for him his accolade.

Now a fountain is a *unit* which is nevertheless twofold, for it consists of an ascending and a descending stream, a resistance and a succumbing, the first active, masculine; the second passive, feminine. Translated into terms of architecture, activity and passivity are epitomized in the vertical member which opposes the gravitational pull, and the horizontal member which submits to it. The Greeks, those superb dramatists, instead of leaving the column a mere cylinder of stone, with a splayed top to increase the bearing surface and lessen the span, made of it a tapered fluted shaft, thus suggesting a powerful, rising force, diminishing as it ascends, and they terminated this shaft with a capital, cushion-shaped or downward-curled, indicative of the yielding of this force to the downward pressure of the lintel.

And having told in this way this story, the tale is continued in the entablature, which the Greeks dramatized in similar fashion. Mr. Pond calls attention to the fact that the forces acting in the entablature are compression above, tension below, while in the middle is a neutral field in which these forces balance one another. Accordingly, in the Ionic entablature the æsthetic intuition of the architect moved him to use in the compressive field the fine-spun lines of tension represented by the fasciæ of the epistyle; the frieze, or neutral zone, he sometimes left plain, sometimes gave over to ornament; but never, in the work of the best period, did he make the mistake of introducing masses or fields of broken light and shade into the lower portion of the entablature as in the cornice (Illustration 1).

The mediæval masonic guilds, after their own fashion, were not less adept than the Greeks at this order of architectural dramatization, and the Gothic cathedrals of the Île de France exhibit as complete and felicitous a showing-forth of the forces at play within their structure as can be found in the world. The architecture was one with the engineering, and the ornament an integral part of the architecture. The pointed arch, which more than anything else may be said to be the norm of Gothic architecture, does not merely *represent* the opposition and equipoise of two diagonally acting forces, but itself *is* such an opposition; and this thrust and counter-thrust, the controlling principle, determines the characteristic forms: the exterior buttresses resist the pressure of the interior vaulting; the pinnacles give an added weight increasing the stability of the buttress; and so it is throughout: the function creates the form, and the form expresses the function. The stone mullions and their tracery were needed in order to give holding and stiffness to the leaded glass; string-courses and cornice moldings took their characteristic shapes from the washes and undercuttings necessary to throw the rain-water clear of the walls; a gargoyle was an ornamented waterspout. And surely nowhere is the fountain-idea more felicitously expressed than in this architecture: exteriorly, in the increasing intricacy and fragility of the towers as they ascend — their *lessening;* interiorly, in the upward sweep of columns and imposts breaking out into the groined vaulting.

The sheer beauty of Greek and Gothic architecture — a *necessitous* beauty — has seduced the latter-day architect into the imitation and employment of their characteristic forms divorced from the functions which they originally subserved and which they so eloquently expressed. But in so doing he violates the most fundamental canon of the architectural art: *the dramatization of structure.* New materials and building methods — not to mention our altered attitude toward life — imperatively demand a new architectural language. The failure to perceive this constitutes the fallacy of the eclectic architect — he who makes a fetish of mere good taste. The tang of his own time, be it acrid or sweet, should flavor everything the architect does; but along with this communication of the immediate, the unique, the special, there should be communicated also some sense of the eternal and the absolute. Saturated as his work may be and should be with the spirit of his own time, it should yet be timeless, as are the pyramids of Egypt, the tragedies of Shakespeare, the paintings of Leonardo. The first of these aims he will achieve by a truthful use of materials and a right expressiveness of use and function; the second, by a dramatization of the *forces* at play within the structure — in brief, the *fountain.* His problem is not basically different from that of the playwright or the novelist, who in presenting the characters and relationships of a group of people in a localized environment, gives an insight into life itself and the essential nature of man and woman.

In most building operations of any magnitude solid masonry has been superseded by steel and re-enforced concrete, but so great is the power of inertia in the world of thought that even in works of engineering the old masonry forms still persist. Here is an example taken from my own experience:

Having been called upon by an eminent bridge engineer to collaborate with him in the designing of a re-enforced concrete bridge, he first made a diagram embodying his idea of the most logical and economical form for it: a series of great semicircular arches supporting a lesser arcade to carry the roadway (A, Illustration 2). It occurred to me when I looked at it that his conception was conditioned by the tyranny of ideas associated with stone construction wherein, for strength and stability, supporting members must perforce be vertical and openings must be arched. But in a manner of construction which is monolithic these necessities do not exist. Accordingly, instead of conveying the weight of the roadway to the main piers by way of vertical supports footing on the arch ring, as is

A
PROPOSED BRIDGE OVER THE DON VALLEY AS ORIGINALLY DESIGNED

B
THE SAME REVISED IN SUCH A WAY AS TO INDICATE THAT IT IS A POURED CONCRETE AND NOT A BUILT-UP MASONRY CONSTRUCTION

2

the universal masonry practice, I suggested that these supports be inclined, like the ribs of a fan, transferring the weight where it needs must be discharged directly, and departing less from the true line of force (B, Illustration 2). My collaborator at first seemed astonished at this suggestion, but the more he thought about it, the better he liked it. The tree-like form was not only more logical, but it was more beautiful, thus verifying anew the dictum that any increase in fitness is an increase in beauty. I myself liked it because it suggested a frozen fountain.

Of the tyranny of old thought-forms the first railway passenger cars and the first automobiles provide a classic illustration, for the former were reproductions of four-in-hand coaches with the addition of flanges to the wheels, and the latter imitated the horse-drawn vehicles of their day. The use of the column, entablature, and arch in steel-frame construction is just such a survival: they have no justification in such construction because they falsify it. The vertical members of a skyscraper, for example, are in effect *continuous,* and the horizontal members, beams though they be for the support of the floors, perform the office of *bracing,* the whole being, in effect, a truss on end, the verticals corresponding to *cords.* The right dramatization of all this may still be open to question, but there can be no doubt about the wrong one: to bedeck such a structure with columns, pilasters, cornices, arches, or other cerements of dead styles is to add lying to stealing. Such things constitute, in this connection, what Sullivan calls "dissenting lines" — as inimical to æsthetic unity of effect as dissenting votes are inimical to political unity.

In the steel-framed building the height of which is less, or not too much greater, than its breadth, it is all right to emphasize the horizontal dimension, thus dramatizing the floor as the important thing, but in a true skyscraper it seems to me that the lines should sweep unbrokenly upward to express the engineering fact of vertical continuity and the poetic fancy of an ascending force in defiance of gravity — a fountain.

But *what goes up must come down:* gravity reasserts itself after the initial impulse is exhausted. A building, however lofty, must end somehow, and the designer's ability is here put to the severest test, and will be measured by the success with which this termination is effected — by the beauty with which his building *dies* on the white counterpane of the sky. In this particular the problem presented by a Gothic cathedral tower is not different from that of a skyscraper, and it is interesting to compare two typical solutions, one mediæval and the other modern (Illustration 3). In the spire of Senlis the transition from the square to the octagon and thence to the pyramid is effected with great subtlety: the angles are filled with miniature towers and spires, and the slender dormers set against the faces of the steeple echo, in their verticality, the tower below, and in their peaked roofs, the spire above, like the ascending and returning waters of a fountain in exquisite reconcilement. John Mead Howells' Pan-Hellenic Hotel suggests no less a frozen fountain, the diminishing force having seemingly to have faltered at those mathematically related stages where the set-backs occur; and, most powerful at the center, the upthrust terminal parallelopipedon finishes in jet-like tracery against the sky. In obedience to a perhaps unconscious intimation on the part of the designer of the building's deeper symbolical significance, he has used the fountain motif in the ornament; moreover, the long vertical piers terminate in logarithmic spirals, suggestive that the rising force returns, fountain-wise, upon itself. The same symbolism is employed in the Ionic and Corinthian capitals, as shown in Illustration 4.

FOUR EXAMPLES OF "BEAUTIFUL DEATHS" IN TERMS OF ARCHITECTURE

4

It would lead only to weariness to multiply examples: these should suffice to make the reader see that even so conditioned and utilitarian an art as architecture, no less than music, poetry, and the drama, may be made to symbolize the life of man as it *should be,* which, like a fountain, is first to prevail and then to fail, but to fail *beautifully:* to meet death in the feminine way, with resignation, as symbolized by the dome; or in the masculine way — like Cyrano, " Steel in my heart and laughter on my lips " — to meet it with defiance, as symbolized by the spire. In either case — bubble or jet — effort and its surcease stand epitomized in the fountain. Music is a fountain of sound, upspringing in *time,* from the still pool of silence. And because all of the arts aspire to the condition of music, architecture attains this most nearly when it suggests the invasion of space by an upthrusting force — a frozen fountain.

SINBAD IN THE CORRIDOR OF FROZEN FOUNTAINS

Sinbad in Main Street of an American City of the Dead.

III
RETROSPECT

THE ARCHITECT'S task — as it is of every artist — over and above the mere business of building, is to mirror the consciousness of his time, striving always to give a nobler aspect to that reflected image, attaining at the same time some expression of the universal through the particular.

Or, to use a different figure, he must make himself an æolian harp of that consciousness, sensitive to every wandering air even while discoursing the music of the spheres — like a pianist playing jazz with one hand and a Gregorian chant with the other and harmonizing them.

Now in order thus to reveal his time it is not necessary to *understand* it — which is fortunate, for that is impossible to anyone as near to it as he. Understanding comes only in retrospect: how much more competently the present might be rendered could it be seen as though it were already the past!

Oddly enough, though, a backward glance in time helps to make clear the present, quite in analogy with the optical fact that to see a given object clearly one should look away from it momentarily at something else. Accordingly let us glance at our immediate architectural past in the light of what we are doing and may do.

I have myself written and published brief retrospects, and the thing has been done by others better qualified; but as I cannot assume the reader's acquaintance with this country's ignominious architectural history, bear with me while I briefly sketch certain of its later phases.

Our present industrial cycle — a merry-go-round sans merriment, already showing signs of running down — began in the period following the Civil War. This was reflected in an architecture even more meaningless and debased than its European prototype. It seems in retrospect the worst architecture in the world — feeble, false, pretentious.

Conditions were improved scarcely at all by the advent of Henry Hobson Richardson, who had a genius for the three-dimensional picturesque. Although he made us architecture-conscious, he was only a flaming comet tracing a hyperbolic orbit and exerting little gravitational pull after he had passed.

In the post-Richardsonian period occurred a revolutionary event of the highest evolutionary importance: the development of the steel frame, supplanting all-masonry construction, and making possible the skyscraper. Almost unnoted, secretly and silently, a method of building which dated from the pyramids was supplanted by something different in kind: walls, instead of supporting, were themselves supported; brick, stone, and concrete became mere fillers and veneers. But architects' trained in the masonry tradition continued to think and design in terms of an order which had passed. They made screen walls look as much as possible like supporting walls, they covered up steel struts and beams with Gothic arches and classic orders, and they even went so far as to resort to concealed steel construction to hold up timbered ceilings and masonry vaulting which could not even support themselves. In brief, architecture abandoned even the pretense of being a dramatization of structure and became mere scene-designing.

Louis Sullivan, a Beaux Arts educated architect, New England born but practicing in Chicago, first and almost alone grasped the full import of the new manner of construction and foresaw its far-reaching effect upon architectural design, though this perception was not achieved completely or at once. Sullivan himself had to go through what he called his "masonry period" in which, like all the others, he temporized and fumbled. But in a series of experiments culminating in the Guaranty (Prudential) Building in Buffalo, New York, he effected, in terms of design, the transition from solid masonry to fire-clay-encased steel. Although his career was not, like Richardson's, triumphant and spectacular, and his creative genius faded before it was fully mature, he became the spiritual father of the skyscraper and wrote himself into architectural history as no other American has.

Meantime, at the World's Columbian Exposition in Chicago, in 1893, the leading architects of the country, men of ability and taste but with a predilection for the old rather than for the new, had everything their own way. Sullivan, to be sure, was given one building, the Transportation, but it was outside the sacred precincts of the Court of Honor, so that nothing untoward should mar the white perfection of that latter-day *Forum Romanum* behind the classic colonnades of which were assembled all the ingenious gadgets and contraptions which the genius of the Machine Age had developed up to that time — Corinthian column cheek by jowl with Baldwin locomotive.

This resuscitation of ancient grandeurs was so bedecked with banners, besplashed by fountains and beblared by bands that instead of being accepted for what it so evidently was — an architectural *tour de force,* a stage-setting pure and simple, an archæological holiday — it was taken seriously as foreshadowing the American City of the Future, and was made the mold into which all official architecture was thereafter cast. The Chicago World's Fair signalized the triumph of eclectic over functional architecture.

Let me here explain that an eclectic architect is one who considers himself free to tell his story in any architectural language he likes; who makes a modern building Greek, Roman, Gothic, Renaissance, for no better reason than that "Agatha loves sunsets"; whose sole arbiter in these matters is what he conceives to be good taste. The functional architect on the other hand believes that architecture is of all arts the most necessitous; that it must mirror the prevailing psychological mood, and that its forms must be determined by function. He is therefore committed to a manner of building in which the stencils of past architectural styles cannot be used.

SINBAD, THE ARTIST, UNDER THE WEIGHT OF PRECEDENT, THE OLD MAN OF THE SEA

Eclecticism, with its facile and specious substitutions of moribund beauty for an honestly attempted expression of the thing which *is,* thus blighted in its bud the only vital and indigenous architectural growth which ever pierced through the American mold — that of Sullivan and his disciples. It delayed our normal evolution and laid its dead hand on nearly every school and college where architecture was taught. Sullivan, the defeated and discredited Great Emancipator, reduced and impoverished, still carried on after his fashion, and shortly before his melancholy death in 1924 wrote *The Autobiography of an Idea,* in which is set down the story of his conflict with the organized forces of conservatism and reaction, a human document of the highest interest and importance.

Frank Lloyd Wright, a pupil but not an imitator of Sullivan, found a measure of release for his highly individual talent in the Middle West and on the Pacific coast. The showing he made there won him the commission to build the Imperial Hotel at Tokyo, thus receiving official recognition by the Japanese government.

RETROSPECT

Although Sullivan and Wright had little influence on American architecture of the post-World's-Fair period — given over almost completely as it was to those forms of eclecticism favored by McKim, Mead and White and other leading practitioners throughout the East — their example was followed in Europe to such purpose that modernistic architecture all the way from the Rhine to Stockholm and Helsingfors is known as "the American style." This came about in the following way:

Certain of the foreign commissioners to the Chicago Exposition, together with visiting European architects, sated with that variety of classicism of which the White City was so luxurious a growth, perversely centered their admiration on Sullivan's Transportation Building, with its golden portal, the like of which they had never seen before. The same fresh note of originality appeared also in his Auditorium Building and Schiller Theatre, and they returned to their own countries with photographs of these buildings and plaster casts of Sullivan's ornament for use in museums and schools. Subsequently drawings and photographs of Wright's work were published in Germany in typographically admirable editions and attracted wide and favorable attention among architects. These influences had an effect analogous to that of Vitruvius upon the architecture of the Italian Renaissance, and of Palladio and Vignole upon English eighteenth-century architecture. That is to say, the modernistic movement in Europe received the stamp of Sullivan and Wright by somewhat the same process and to something the same extent that Italian Renaissance architecture received the stamp of Imperial Rome and English Renaissance architecture of Italy; and although the modernistic movement in Europe has advanced on lines of its own, that stamp remains indelible.

Indeed, this European trend toward organic or functional architecture (in contradistinction to traditional or eclectic) is of such vitality and has grown to such proportions that it is now producing important repercussions in the United States, the land of its birth — or perhaps it would be more correct to say that the same forces which operated there are now operating here, the only difference being a difference in *time*. Be that as it may, the modernistic movement in America today, interesting and full of promise as it undoubtedly is, does not appear to be based upon such well-thought-out ideas and deeply held convictions as have gone to the shaping of its European correlative. It is therefore under suspicion of being just another twist which eclecticism has taken — the latest architectural *fashion* rather than the first strivings toward a *style*.

One knows what privation and suffering Sullivan went through for the sake of his Idea; one is sure that Wright and Le Corbusier — whom I take as representative of the European functionalists — would make any renunciation rather than build counter to those principles which they advocate and which they try to make their buildings represent, but the chief practitioners of latter-day American modernism, though they may seem to be doing the same sort of thing, and doing it with even greater expertness, appear to be under no such compulsion; they turn aside, they wink the other eye on occasion, like augurs ministering to a religion in which they believe, not because they cannot help it, but because it is both fashionable and profitable. They are still eclectics according to the strict definition of the term. The *true* functionalist, on the other hand, is rooted in an idea to which it is impossible for him ever to be false; he must try at all times and at all costs to honor with use those first principles upon which the architectural art is founded — principles which, however various their application, suffer no change from age to age.

ARCHITECTURE OF THE GENERAL GRANT PERIOD

SKYSCRAPERS, MEDIAEVAL AND MODERN—TIME'S REVERSAL OF SACRED AND PROFANE

IV
THE SKYSCRAPER

OF ALL our architectural flora, the skyscraper alone is truly indigenous to the American soil. Our churches, our court houses, libraries, museums, banks, are for the most part uninspired adaptations of stale European originals, but the skyscraper is *a natural growth,* and a symbol of the American spirit in its more obvious aspect — that ruthless, tireless, assured *energism,* delightedly proclaiming, " What a great boy am I! " The skyscraper is important both as an architectural and as a social manifestation; let us therefore seek to discover and define those forces and influences which have shaped and are in process of shaping it as it exists today.

On the social and economic forces I shall not dwell further than to remove a few misconceptions. It is popularly supposed that the skyscraper arose as the result of the impossibility of lateral expansion, lower Manhattan with its confining rivers and the Chicago Loop (the districts where these buildings first shot skyward) often being cited in proof of this. But the so-called Loop is not a nature-made, but a man-made barrier —

metaphysical, not physical — while an aerial view of New York reveals at a glance large tracts of low-lying buildings in and around the Wall Street district which if built to the height of a few more stories, would accommodate a population vastly larger than the skyscrapers harbor. It is a fact that the average height of buildings on Manhattan island is lower than that of most European capitals where the skyscraper is a thing unknown — they have a greater population per acre than New York.

The *raison d'être* of the skyscraper is therefore not physical but psychological: it arose in answer to the desire of the herd to become a super-herd — of spot-cards to become face-cards. Skyscrapers appear only and always on those sacred acres which for some mysterious reason have become the blue heaven of the business man. High buildings in preferred areas owe their existence to exactly the same cause as high prices for front-row seats at a show.

But from another point of view the skyscraper came into being as the result of an effort to get the better of the real-estate agent and the tax collector by expanding in the free dimension, capturing and turning to profit more than an equitable share of air and sunlight. Ugly as the word may sound, the skyscraper is a product of human greed, thus standing in ideal symbolic relation to the country and to the times. I hasten to add, however, that this motive is no more ignoble than those which have inspired architectural masterpieces canonized by universal acclamation and sanctified by time. Motives — even one's own — will not bear too close examination. Some of the most magnificent products of the building impulse throughout the ages were inspired by emotions far different than those which they excite in the beholder: for example, blood-lust — witness the Colosseum; fear of invasion — witness the Great Wall of China; personal pride — witness the Mausoleum of Hadrian; the love of luxury — witness the Thermæ of Caracalla. And so one might go on; the littleness of the motive is lost sight of in the greatness of the monument, just as the hook and bait which landed him is swallowed up in Leviathan. This is all part of the universal paradox, so disconcerting to our moralities: the favorite food of epicures springs from the dung-hill, and from ground richly manured by dollars spring sky-piercing Valhallas crowned with light. It militates not at all against the skyscraper that in the last analysis it is a product of sharp practice, an enclosure for the transaction of sharp bargains, so long as we do not kid ourselves into calling it a Cathedral of Commerce and try to make it look like something other than it is. Hypocrisy in architecture is successful only with the undiscerning, while simple honesty somehow always satisfies and gives forth overtones of beauty.

PHYSICAL FACTORS

Of the physical factors which have gone to the shaping of the skyscraper the first, and of the first importance, is steel-frame construction — that system of riveted-together vertical and horizontal members insuring strength, lightness, rigidity, stability; a skyscraper being, as said before, a truss placed upright. Co-equal with this in the sense that vertical building would have been impossible without it is the fast, safe passenger elevator — the very piston of the machine. And the bringing of this to its present state of perfection involved mechanical difficulties far greater than the mere piling of story upon story, once the trick was learned. Mention must also be made of the ingenious methods now in use for the sinking of foundations to great depths, for without this Chicago could never have stretched its neck as high as New York, the early Chicago skyscrapers having been floated on rafts, so to speak, on a lake of mud, with perilous results. And, finally, the draining, heating, lighting, water-, fire-, and wind-proofing of these buildings had to be competently taken care of in order to make them possible. The aggregate of inventive and mechanical ability involved in the production of a modern American skyscraper is perhaps greater than in any other work of man.

A conditioning factor in skyscraper construction has arisen in certain localities in recent years through legislative action designed to diminish encroachments upon the ethical rights of property owners and the right of everyone to a modicum of light and air. In New York this has resulted in the set-back type of skyscraper. The French Mansard roof was the product of a similar necessity — legislative, not structural or æsthetic. Occasionally, by a glossing of the crass fact of this necessity, or by making a virtue of it — such as transforming the set-backs into hanging gardens — the effect has been good, yielding less monotonous outlines and a greater play of light and shade; but without skilled treatment of some sort these buildings have the look of gigantic bureaus with partly pulled-out drawers.

ÆSTHETIC FACTORS

It will be clear from the foregoing that the skyscraper has been shaped and developed by practical, not æsthetic necessity: like a bridge, though in a lesser degree, it is an engineering problem. The engineer has performed his part magnificently, because American engineers are the most daring and competent in the world — they have to be, by reason of the demands made upon them. The architect, on the other hand (and what I say holds good whether engineer and architect be two men or a single individual with a dual talent) has misconceived his problem, which is not to *adorn* the necessitous engineering structure, nor to translate it into this or that dead architectural language, but to *dramatize* it. Sullivan was the first architect to face the problem from this viewpoint, and his was therefore the prime important æsthetic influence, even though during the period of his activity the skyscraper as a cloud-piercing obelisk did not exist.

Sullivan's contribution consisted in demonstrating by eloquent precept and a few admirable examples that a steel frame encased within a protecting fire-clay envelope need not and should not be made to look as though the walls were of solid masonry, supporting the weight of the floors as well as their own weight; because they support neither, he treated the walls frankly as a veneer. Furthermore, he made the tall building " a proud and soaring thing " by emphasizing and optically increasing its height by the use of long, unbroken vertical lines, thus forever putting an end to the ridiculous practice of piling the classic orders on top of one another like a house of cards, common up to the time of his innovation. That anything so obvious should need to be innovated seems incomprehensible now, but it is a fact that the schoolmen exercised their ingenuity to *diminish* the height of the first tall buildings by means of horizontal string-courses, entablatures, cornices, and other devices. The Condit Building, in New York, one of Sullivan's lesser-known designs (Illustration 5), though it looks conservative enough in the light of later developments, represents a radical departure from then current methods.

Viollet-le-Duc in his *Discourses on Architecture* affirms that it is the business of the architect " to fulfil with scrupulous exactness all the conditions imposed by necessity, and to employ materials with due regard to their qualities and capacities." Sullivan laid firm hold of the fact that new materials and building methods demand new architectural forms for their expression: " It is my belief," he wrote, " that it is of the very essence of every problem that it contains its own solution." And having stated the problem of the tall office building in winged words, he solved it in ponderable materials, even going so far as to invent a style of ornament appropriate to and expressive of the nature of baked clay. He did this so successfully that it was regarded by his contemporaries as his most important contribution to an American style, much to Sullivan's chagrin, who saw his ornament being imitated and his sound architectural ideas ignored. It was this, perhaps, which prompted him to declare that it would be to our æsthetic good if we should refrain entirely from the use of ornament for a period of years in order that our thoughts might be concentrated acutely upon the production of buildings " well formed and comely in the nude."

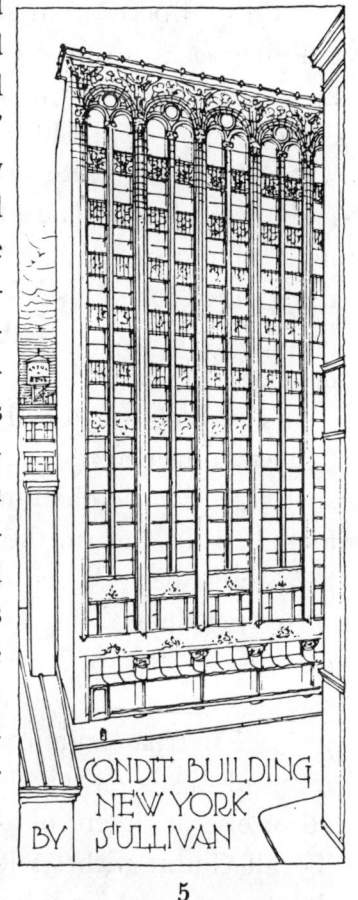

CONDIT BUILDING
NEW YORK
BY SULLIVAN

5

This statement alone reveals his greatness, coming as it does from the finest inventor of ornament we have produced. Like a mountain the magnitude of which becomes apparent only as one recedes from it in space, we are beginning to realize Sullivan's true greatness as we recede from him in time. He was the first American modernist, prophet and precursor of the small best that is being done today under that banner; and, engulfed as he was in the great bromidic tide, he cracked the hard shell of our complacency and was an inspiration to certain young men of his day. As Charles Whitaker says of him, " He was a flash of beauty in the dull and deadly world of the American draughting room of his day, where copyists slaved over plates and photographs under the delusion that they were practicing the art of building."

Cass Gilbert, an architect of great ability, but not so bold and deep a thinker as Sullivan, conceived of the skyscraper as a Cathedral of Commerce. The Woolworth Building and the New York Life Building are embodiments of this idea. He argued, probably, as follows: Today we make a religion of business; therefore why not treat the mart more or less like a temple, lavishing upon it all our best? The Gothic style lends itself admirably to modern uses, for it is pre-eminently *vertical,* the very thing called for in a skyscraper; moreover, it is infinitely flexible, adapted to all uses, and unencumbered by canons of proportion as the classic orders are.

The Woolworth Building, which struck this new keynote, is certainly " in every inch a proud and soaring thing " and remains today in many respects the finest embodiment of the skyscraper idea. It so stimulated the architects throughout the country to emulation and to imitation that Gilbert's must be reckoned the next important influence after Sullivan's on skyscraper design. But in spite of the admirable quality of his work as regards disposition of parts, line, and mass, and more than all else its essential *practicality,* it is based on false premises so far as the use of Gothic forms and ornamentation is concerned. We do not and cannot think in terms of mediævalism; therefore logic prescribes either no ornament at all or else ornament of a kind consistent with our particular psychology. To fill Gothic niches with effigies of noted scientists and captains of industry instead of disciples and saints and to substitute dollar signs for symbols of the Trinity is a ridiculously wrong answer to the problem. Not that Gilbert was ever guilty of just that, but his imitators have been. The necessity for an altogether new ornamental mode cannot be evaded or escaped, because it is inherent. But that is a thing of slow growth, the product, usually, of many minds; it cannot be created overnight, and in the meantime what is the poor architect to do? The only answer appears to be: string your own bead necklace, however crude, or else go bare — give over the rifling of European graveyards in any case.

The next important influence after Gilbert's came in a strange way and from a strange source: "The Loser Wins" might be the title of its story.

The Chicago Tribune Building (Illustration 6), widely advertised as the most beautiful skyscraper in the world, was built according to the design submitted by John Mead Howells and Raymond Hood in a world-wide competition of which they were the winners. It is in a pseudo-Gothic style, a piece of magnificent but irrelevant stage scenery, the limestone casing made to look as picturesquely mediæval as possible, the crowning lantern flanked by flying buttresses which cast interesting shadows but do not buttress, being like hands pressed to a bewildered head engaged in thinking, "So this is Chicago! How did I get here, I wonder."

THE PICTURESQUE AND THE UTILITARIAN: THE CHICAGO TRIBUNE BUILDING AND THE NEW YORK EVENING NEWS BUILDING

6

The second prize design, by Eliel Saarinen, a Finnish architect, was as different as possible from that of his successful rivals: simple, direct, unpretentious, with a square tower which just *stopped,* but with an indefinable felicity, by reason of subtle diminishments.

Sullivan hailed this design as a return to, and a carrying forward of, those principles of which he had been the advocate and exemplar; Bertram Goodhue, himself a competitor, who had had an advance view of all the drawings, told me that Saarinen's design was in a class by itself and superior to all the others, and such was the consensus of opinion, professional and lay. Observe the workings of poetic justice: though the victory was theirs, and the spoils of victory in good American dollars, the winners themselves were convicted of sin and suffered conversion. For what other inference can be drawn from the appearance of the New York Evening News Building (Illustration 6), by these same architects, which is quite in the spirit of Saarinen's design and as unlike their own previous effort as can well be imagined? Destitute of ornament except about the entrance, and of any architectural grace save its soaring verticals and the finely disposed, proportionately related parts, this building somehow succeeds in making its neighbors, the Chrysler and the Chanin buildings, look a little bit silly by comparison. It does not seem to stand on tiptoe blowing a silver trumpet, as does the one, nor to give a false effect of massiveness, as does the other, by means of squat pilasters and artificial buttresses. It assumes to be only what it is: a work of engineering, a cliff-like human hive, a monster of the mere market.

Saarinen's influence on skyscraper architecture has been pronounced, particularly in Chicago, where his formula has been much followed, although he merely brought to a focus certain tendencies which had already been making themselves felt: simple rectilinear masses, the verticals rising sheer without dissenting lines, the elimination of cornices, and a general absence of ornament except it be *integral,* in contradistinction to *applied.*

The final influence to be noted is that of Hugh Ferris, who is not in the strict sense an architect at all, but an architectural " renderer." His architectural sense and his æsthetic sensitiveness are, however, so superior to that of most of the architects who employ him to make pictures of their buildings that it is often highly disillusioning to compare his drawings with their originals, though the architect's was of course the enormously more difficult problem.

Ferris served his masters so well that he himself enslaved some of them, judging by the increasing tendency to make skyscrapers look as much as possible like his imaginative drawings. His book, *The Metropolis of Tomorrow,* appears to be exerting an influence on skyscraper design analogous to that which Piranesi's prison etchings exercised upon George Dance's design for Old Newgate. Turning the pages of this book we may read not only the last skyscraping word, but the one which has not yet been uttered. Both Ferris and Wright have conceived of the skyscraper of the future as having walls of metal and glass, *hung,* as it were, from the steel framework. Ferris not only shows pictures of such a building, but a model of it stands in his office; and Wright's working drawings of his own conception of an all glass and metal skyscraper have already been published in the architectural magazines.

Such a next step would be entirely consistent and logical: glass is one of the few building materials still in process of development, and there has been an increasing tendency to increase window area at the expense of wall-surface. A building all of shining metal and glass would constitute a more honest dramatization of the essential nature of the skyscraper than those now in vogue, since it is not, in essence, a masonry structure, though always made to appear as though it were. The lofty rectilinear steel frames of skyscrapers outlined in sable and orange against the cerulean New York sky are to me always a marvel and a delight; but no sooner have they put on their masonry overcoats than the chief element of their charm has vanished — that *strong lightness*. So strong are they that their structural limit of height far overpasses the economic limit, and so light are they that the finished edifice weighs less than the rock removed to give it foothold and cellarage. Because they are thus strong and light it is part of the business of the architect to make them look so, but this appears to be the last thing that occurs to him to do. On the contrary he continues to try to make them look as heavy and spineless as possible. The Woolworth Building gives something of the desired impression; also, by reason of its shining verticals, the Empire State Building tower. The idea, however, is probably capable of still more eloquent expression.

SOCIAL FACTORS

Having traced the evolution of the skyscraper even beyond the point at which it stands today, I might here make an end, but this survey would be superficial did I not now continue in a somewhat different strain.

An incorrigible symbolist, I cannot but attach symbolical significance to the fact that one may turn page after page of *The Metropolis of Tomorrow* without coming upon a single human figure: here is pictured a world from which humanity appears to have perished, done to death by the successful realization of its own egregious dream. The skyscraper, that latest and greatest product of human power and ingenuity, is essentially inhuman, not because its construction exacts the toll of a workman killed for every story erected, but because it has arisen in defiance of the common rights of common humanity, and this disregard will probably in the end achieve its doom.

For if these buildings continue to multiply as they are now multiplying, traffic congestion — for which they are directly responsible — will become traffic paralysis and conditions will be created not unlike those shown in the German cinema *Metropolis,* wherein everyone lives and works, in effect, underground, except the overlords, who have pre-empted the right to breathe the free air and look upon the sky. The skyscraper's advantage is gained at the expense of its more lowly neighbor, but when the owners of the surrounding property avail themselves of their inalienable right to themselves build skyscrapers, no one benefits; unnatural and intolerable conditions, impossible to overcome, are the inevitable result.

But under more drastic initial restrictions which might conceivably be imposed, the advantages — practical, economic, æsthetic — of this manner of vertical expansion might be made good use of, for they are many, and too great to be forgone. Such advantages can be insured only under conditions long familiar to every student of the science of cities, but they are apparently impossible of fulfilment short of a social revolution or a complete change of heart on the part of almost everyone concerned. As Le Corbusier, Ferris, and others before them have made plain, skyscrapers should be erected only at focal points where traffic lanes converge, and the surrounding buildings should be kept relatively low and sufficiently distant; or else broad avenues, flanked by high buildings, should alternate with narrower streets flanked by low ones; in this way light and air for all would be assured. But it is obvious that under the existing governmental and social regime, property laws, and system of land-ownership, such solutions will continue to remain only a city-planner's dream.

A city ought to be a garden and not a jungle: One night as I sat watching from the roof of the Hotel Shelton a great fish-shaped balloon swimming about in the blue void above the tops of the buildings I was momentarily subject to the illusion that they were all weedy growths at the bottom of some gigantic aquarium, so unrelated to reason and order did they seem.

But putting aside all sociological, moralistic, and narrowly æsthetic considerations, if we look at these megatheria of commerce with something of the same detachment and young-eyed wonder that we are able to bring to the contemplation of the Pyramids — to which they are related as life to death — we shall see these buildings most truly. So great is our immersion, however, in the medium which produced them, that this is more difficult for us than for the foreigner visiting our shores. A world-battered, hard-boiled Englishman confessed to me that his first vision of the towers of Manhattan, sun-illumined above the low-lying Atlantic mist, moved him to tears for some reason which he could not understand; and a cynical but sensitive Frenchman on beholding the same sight was heard to murmur, " *C'est beau, c'est grand, c'est vrai!* "

Such emotion, such enthusiasm does them honor, and is far finer than our own unimaginative acceptance of what is surely the eighth wonder of the world. Silhouetted against the grey of dawn, the crimson of sunset, or bright with the pellucid radiance of mid-day; rain-drenched, mist-enveloped, or piercing the darkness with late-lighted windows and shining coronets of flame, these campanili of the New Feudalism, however base-born and æsthetically uninspired, are none the less the planet's most august and significant symbol of proud-spirited man, " flashing unquenched defiance to the stars."

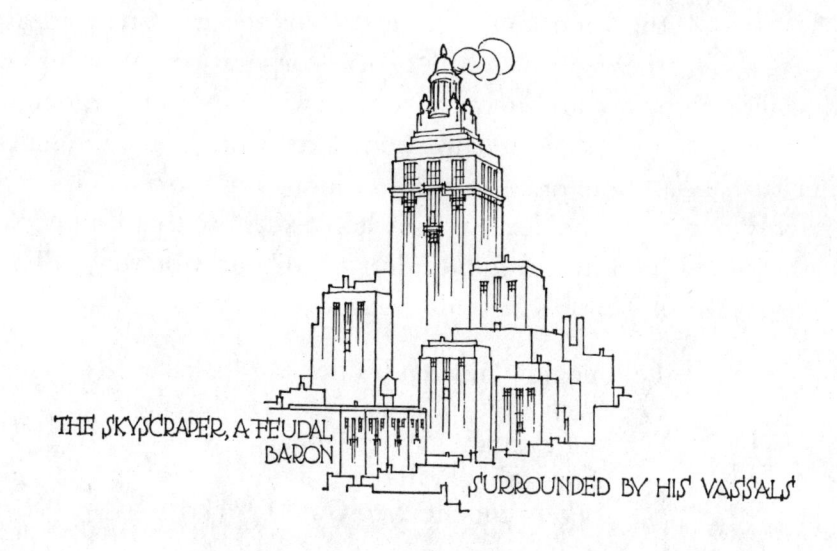

THE SKYSCRAPER, A FEUDAL BARON SURROUNDED BY HIS VASSALS

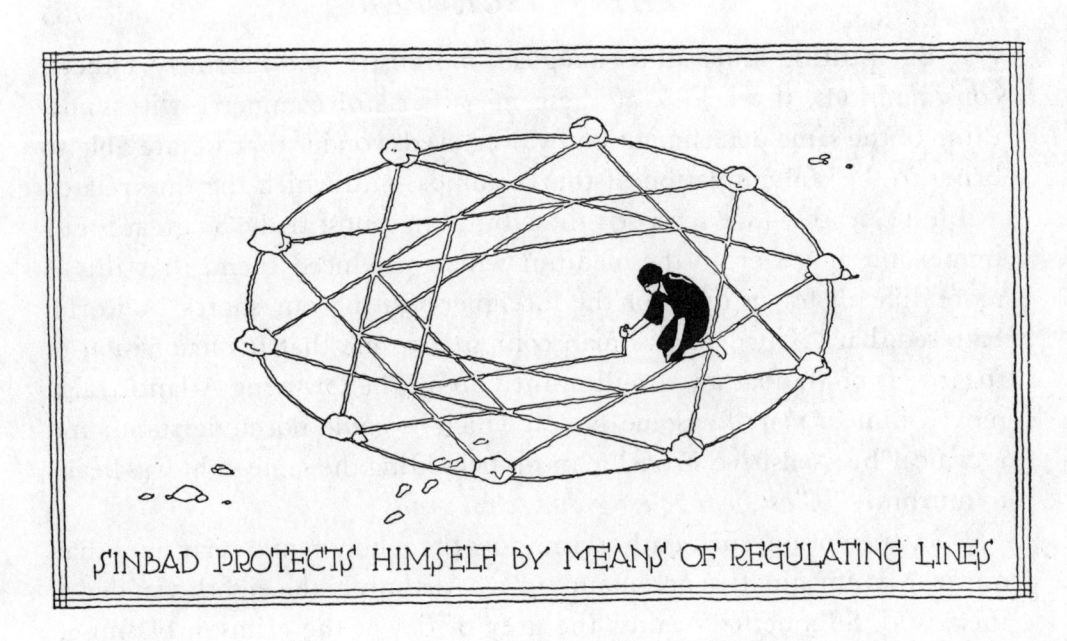

SINBAD PROTECTS HIMSELF BY MEANS OF REGULATING LINES

V
REGULATING LINES

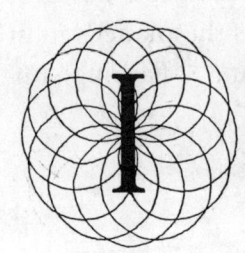

I HAVE dwelt at such length upon the skyscraper because it is so accurate a mirror of the national consciousness, reflecting as it does our irrepressible energy, our love of *bigness,* our predatory habit, and the triumph — for the time being, at least — of the industrial ideal over the agricultural: of the corporation over the grange. Besides, it is the only architectural entity which has undergone a consistent evolution in a definite direction: Everything else represents only another turn in a circle of ephemeral fashions reminiscent of some past never truly our own and leading nowhere except to that limbo wherein are gathered the architectural blunders of all our yesterdays. To paraphrase a stanza of Villon's famous ballade:

> Tell me now in what hidden way is
>   Carpenter's Classic, Wooden Greek.
> What of Eastlake? Where today is
>   The Italian Villa farm-house freak?
>   Where for the Neo-Gothic seek?

REGULATING LINES

> With Richardson Romanesque I fear
> > They are gone the way of the sham antique —
> Oh where are the styles of yester-year?

But this merry-go-round could not go on revolving endlessly, and after a few more turns, represented by McKim, Mead and Whitism, Beaux Artism, Austro-Urbanistic Modernism, we are at last headed in the direction of true functionalism: toward the development of an architecture which shall be above all things indigenous and organic. This tendency, first revealed in the skyscraper, is of fast-gathering momentum; it is even manifest in the architectural schools and colleges, those strongholds of conservatism. While it is true, as said before, that the movement here is under suspicion of being only another twist which eclecticism has taken, it can now never turn backward to mere copyism of the past.

Confronted with some of the sins committed in the name of the new architectural liberty, it is impossible not to yield to apprehension, and even to regret. But this is futile: the wild and wanton experimentation of the ignorant and incompetent, freed of all restraint, is an inescapable phase we must go through. Having thrown away his water-wings of precedent, either the tyro must learn to swim or he must drown. This book has been written in the hope that it may aid and inspire those who are struggling in these perilous seas forlorn; so, having given that backward glance so clarifying to forward vision, I shall proceed to a discussion of *regulating lines*.

A work of architecture may be significant, organic, dramatic, but it will fail of being a work of art unless it be also *schematic*. What is the meaning of this word in this connection?

It means a systematic disposition of parts according to some co-ordinating principle. Only by *schematization* can multiplicity be resolved into unity, and unity split up into multiplicity without itself being lost in the process: like the string in a pearl necklace, or the movement of the baton of an orchestra-leader, schematization is an agent of unity, the preserver of union.

In decorative and pictorial art *a color scheme* — some principle according to which colors have been chosen, disposed, and proportioned —

is an agent of schematization, an aid to unity. In music the key, or chosen series of notes in which a piece is written, also its division into beats, measures, and bars, operate to the same end. Quite in analogy with this selective process, and the dividing of time into larger and lesser units, *space* should be similarly divided and subdivided as a means of schematization in architectural design.

And because the architect usually develops his idea first in plan and in two dimensions, this subdivision will be most easily effected by the use of what is called *profile paper*, a surface marked off into larger and lesser squares. By means of these *regulating lines* the designer is easily able to establish parallelograms whose interrelations, co-ordinated by numerical ratios of small magnitude, are harmonious, a source of subjective satisfaction in themselves. The *unit of measurement* may correspond to the foot, the yard, the meter, but preferably it should have some relation to man himself — his stature (equal to his span), the length of his pace, his foot, his hand. For this insures that the work be on the human scale, that it shall conform to the human rhythm — just as music is related to inhalation and exhalation, to the heart-beat, or to the tread of marching men.

This use of linear units as an aid to schematization is one aspect of what is known as *static symmetry*. It is the most obvious and easily achieved method of binding the elements of a work of architecture together in an invisible mathematical net. Although not honored in these days by a sufficient observance, it has been practiced the world over from far back. The enclosures built by primitive man were frequently governed by such elementary calculation, no less than the works of the greatest architects, as measurements made from them as well as surviving drawings sufficiently attest (Illustration 7).

" The regulating line," says Le Corbusier, " is a satisfaction of a spiritual order which leads to the pursuit of ingenious and harmonious relations. It confers on the work the quality of rhythm."

Now there is an order of regulating lines other than that derived from the use of linear units, more subtle, and at the same time more simple. It consists in the co-ordination of the elements of a design by means of such elementary geometrical figures as the circle, the equilateral triangle, and

REGULATING LINES

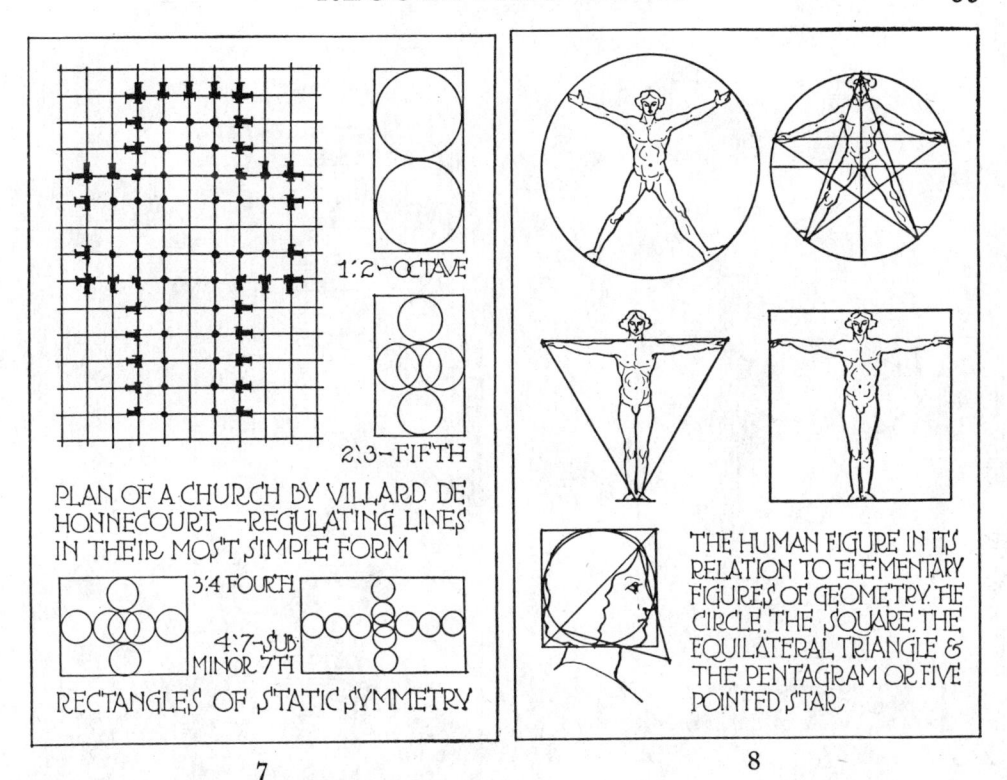

PLAN OF A CHURCH BY VILLARD DE HONNECOURT—REGULATING LINES IN THEIR MOST SIMPLE FORM

1:2—OCTAVE
2:3—FIFTH
3:4 FOURTH
4:7—SUB MINOR 7TH

RECTANGLES OF STATIC SYMMETRY

THE HUMAN FIGURE IN ITS RELATION TO ELEMENTARY FIGURES OF GEOMETRY: THE CIRCLE, THE SQUARE, THE EQUILATERAL TRIANGLE & THE PENTAGRAM OR FIVE POINTED STAR

7   8

the square (the two dimensional correlatives of the sphere, the tetrahedron, and the cube). Their employment for this purpose yields "a satisfaction of a spiritual order" perhaps on account of their *archetypal* character, the archetypal world being the spiritual world. Why or in what sense these figures are archetypal I need not go into here; suffice it to say that the circle, the equilateral triangle, and the square are regulating lines in the architecture of the human temple itself, as Illustration 8 shows at a glance.

Other regulating lines sometimes used are the right-angled isosceles triangle and the so-called " Egyptian " triangle, an isosceles triangle having a ratio of base to altitude as eight to five; also, the Pythagorean " marriage " triangle, whose sides are represented by the numbers three, four, and five, used anciently — and even today — for the establishment of a right angle. These triangles lend themselves to the uses of schematization for the reason that the mathematical relations between their parts are simple and significant.

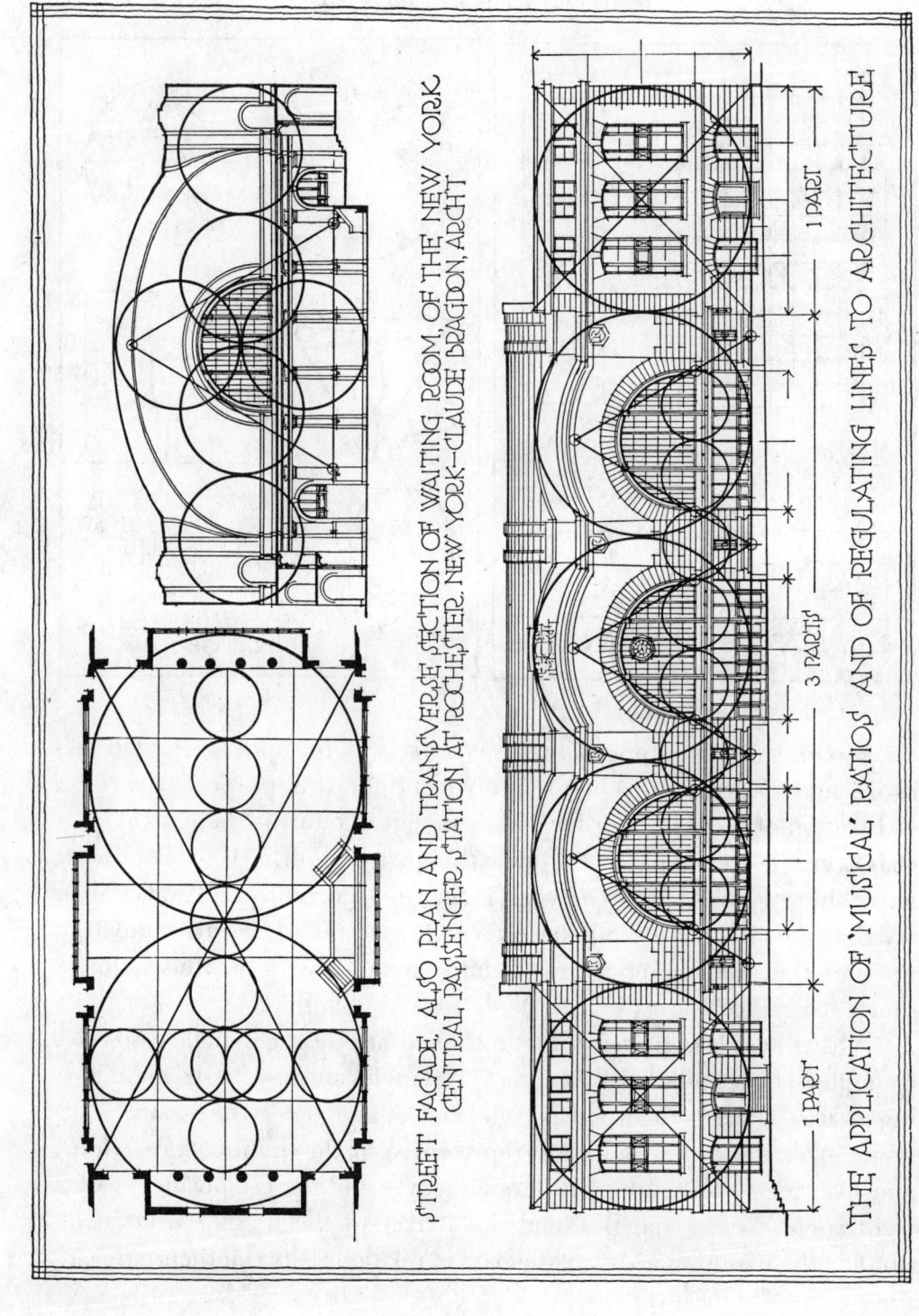

STREET FAÇADE, ALSO PLAN AND TRANSVERSE SECTION OF WAITING ROOM, OF THE NEW YORK CENTRAL PASSENGER STATION AT ROCHESTER, NEW YORK—CLAUDE BRAGDON, ARCH'T

1 PART   3 PARTS   1 PART

THE APPLICATION OF 'MUSICAL' RATIOS AND OF REGULATING LINES TO ARCHITECTURE

REGULATING LINES

If a work of architecture is, in the well-known phrase, "frozen music," it is so only by reason of a harmonious relation subsisting between its various parts — otherwise it is only frozen noise. A realization of this fact prompted me to try to determine the important proportions of the New York Central railway station at Rochester, New York, by means of numerical ratios expressing the consonant intervals in music — more particularly the octave, the fifth, the subminor seventh, 1 : 2, 2 : 3, 4 : 7 — in conjunction with the square, the circle, and the equilateral triangle. Illustration 9 indicates the way in which this was done. The length of the waiting-room, measured on the floor, is twice its width, and the height (from window to window) is half the width. The parallelogram defined by the walls above the floor is slightly more subtle, the ratio being 4 : 7. Five equal circles — remotely suggestive of the driving wheels of some giant locomotive — establish the main divisions of the façade, three being given to the waiting-room, and one to each of the wings, which thus define squares. This ratio between the ends and the center, 2 : 3, expresses the musical interval of the fifth, and the octave (1 : 2) occurs in the façade also, in the relation of the principal voids to the principal solids, since the great windows are twice as broad as the piers which separate them. An equilateral triangle is the determining factor in certain subdivisions both of the waiting-room and the façade, the top of the wainscot being used as a base line in the one case, and the top of the water-table in the other; for it may be stated as a general rule that whenever three important points of a composition coincide (approximately or exactly) with the three vertices of an equilateral triangle, it makes for beauty of proportion.

The employment of *parallel diagonals* as regulating lines constitutes another easily applied and useful method of relating the various parts of a design to one another: The principal mass, either in plan or in elevation, being expressed by a rectangle, the diagonal of that rectangle and its perpendicular become the measure of such secondary elements as pavilions, wings, doors, windows, etc. Parallel diagonals establish parallelograms of different sizes but expressed by the same ratios, and in architectural design yield results analogous to those laws which appear to govern bodily structure whereby a long, thin person has attenuated hands and feet, whereas if the figure be short and stout, these members will correspond with it (Illustration 10).

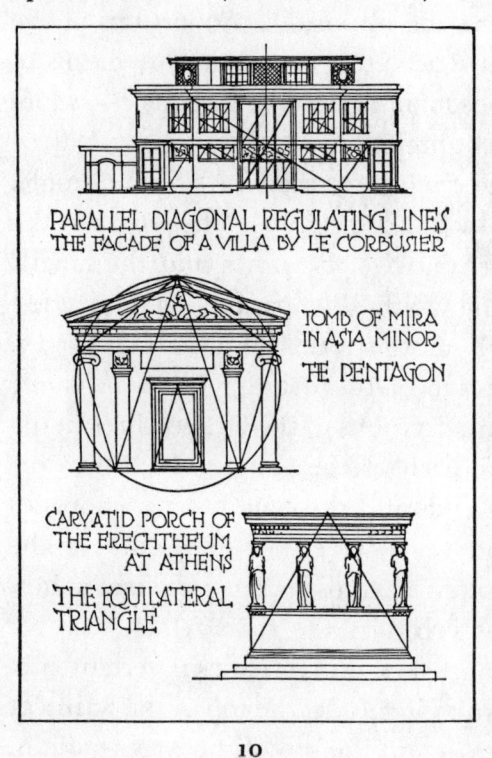

It must not be thought that these aids to schematization by means of regulating lines are mutually exclusive: they can be made to work together like balls in the hand of a skilful juggler, but the manner and extent of their use must be determined by each one for himself. A building planned and proportioned in accordance with geometrical synopses of this order will have the appearance of being well and reasonably made, well unified, well modulated, not the product of chance or capriciousness. Mathematical law, having permeated it, will shine through it, just as it does through the creations of nature, which are nothing if not mathematical.

DYNAMIC SYMMETRY

The foregoing aids to schematization all come under the general head of *static symmetry*. There is, however, another system of regulating lines known as dynamic symmetry, with which the name of Jay Hambidge is indissolubly associated because discovered — or, as he claims, *rediscovered* — and developed by him. Howard Giles, one of its best-known living exponents, defines dynamic symmetry as a system for controlling space relations — a means whereby are achieved related areas or spaces. It is more subtle than the linear-unit system in that it involves the next higher dimension, and more *vital* on account of its close accord with certain phenomena of natural growth. The manner of its application to problems of design is in general not different from that already shown for static symmetry: the main elements are determined by rectangles possessing special mathematical properties, their diagonals, the perpendiculars to the diagonals, and the lesser space-relations which inevitably follow from the subdivision of the rectangles in this way.

SINDBAD FORCES THE LOGARITHMIC SPIRAL TO DISGORGE ITS TREASURE

When Mr. Hambidge told me that the logarithmic spiral — "*Spira Mirabilis,*" as it has been called — was at the root of dynamic symmetry, I had to believe in it at once, for of all geometric figures whatsoever this is the most ubiquitous, being indeed the unit-form of nature. If astronomers are right in thinking the nebulæ to be stellar systems like our own, because of the shape which these assume, the logarithmic spiral may be the archetypal pattern of the cosmos itself.

This curve, because it makes equal angles with all radii drawn through its origin, is known as the equi-angular or constant-angle spiral. It was first described mathematically by Descartes. It is seen in the snail's shell and in the ram's horn, they being the result of a process of continued proportionate growth. Conceive of this spiral therefore as a cone rolled up on itself: a snail's shell is such a rolled-up cone.

A marvelous law of proportion is inherent in the logarithmic spiral: when any three radii vectors are drawn, equi-angular distance apart, the middle one is a mean proportional between the other two. This is evidenced and made available for æsthetic uses by translating the spiral from a curved form into an angular one, as shown in A, Illustration 11. From this it is but a step to the creation of a series of rectangles the diagonals and the perpendiculars to the diagonals of which are radii vectors at right angles to one another. This yields a double series of lines in continued proportion, each line bearing the same relation to its predecessor as the one following bears to it. So far as design is concerned, the curve of the spiral can be dispensed with, but though gone, let it not be forgotten; its felt presence imparts to dynamically symmetrical compositions their indefinable satisfactoriness. It is well to insist on this point, for, immersed in a forest of "root-rectangles," "reciprocals," "whirling squares," and the like, there is danger of not seeing the wood for the trees, and so missing the austere and elegant simplicity of the whole system.

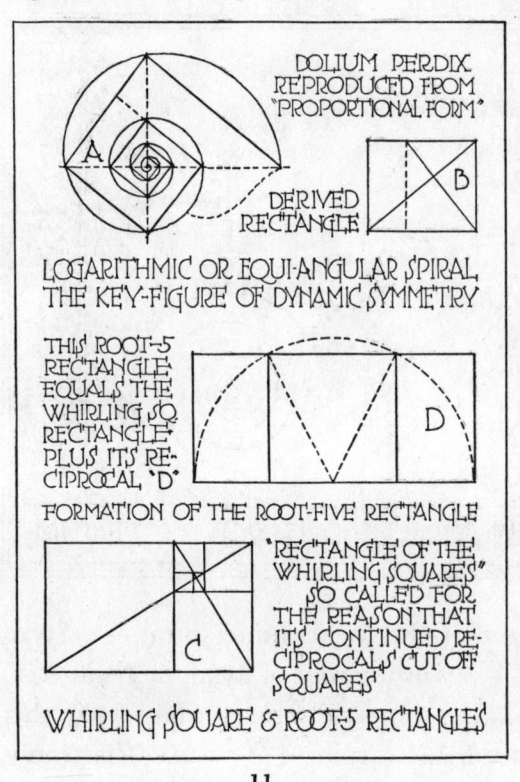

Let us now proceed to the consideration of the rectangles themselves. They are called root-rectangles because although in general their ends and sides are incommensurable with one another *linearly,* the *squares* on the ends and sides *are* commensurable and expressible by quantitatively small ratios. The names root-two, root-three, root-four, and root-five have been applied to these rectangles for the reason that the square on the end is respectively one half, one third, one fourth, and one fifth of the area of the square on the side. The ratios expressing the relation of width to length will accordingly be: unity to the square root of two, of three, of four, and of five ($1 : \sqrt{2}$, $1 : \sqrt{3}$, $1 : \sqrt{4}$, $1 : \sqrt{5}$). These rectangles constitute the beginning of an infinite series, but dynamic

REGULATING LINES

symmetry does not make use of any beyond the fourth — the root-five rectangle.

All root-rectangles have the following properties in common, besides the commensurability of their squares: The perpendicular to the diagonal, prolonged until it meets the long side of the rectangle, is itself the diagonal of a reciprocal rectangle similar to the whole; repeated within the rectangle, these exhaust the area without a remainder. Lines drawn parallel with the sides of the rectangle through (a) the intersection of the perpendicular to the diagonal and the long side, and (b) through the intersection of the diagonal with its perpendicular (the "eye" of the spiral), yield rectangles similar to the whole and exhaust the area without a remainder. All this, confusing in verbal description, is clear

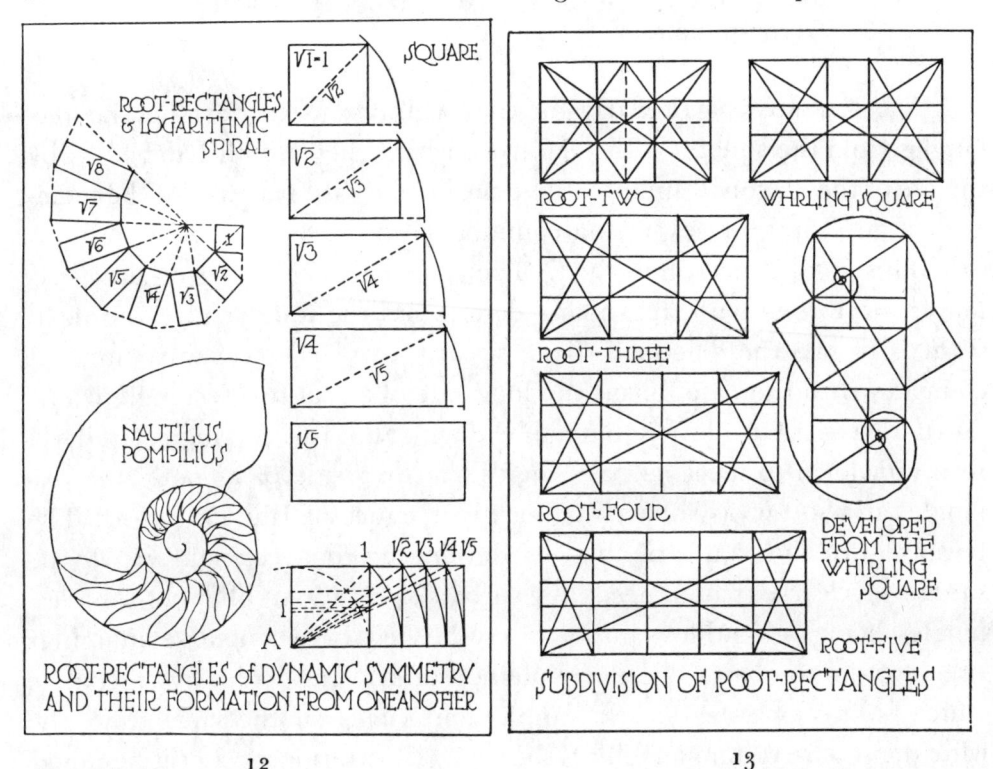

12   13

at a glance at Illustrations 12 and 13. It is by reason of these mathematical properties that root-rectangles are so satisfactory to the eye and so useful to the designer.

In addition to the first four root-rectangles, dynamic symmetry makes use of another, the rectangle of the whirling squares, so called because its continued reciprocals (C, Illustration 11) establish squares within the rectangle. It is in a way a derivative of the root-five rectangle, to which it is closely related.

Let us next learn how to construct these various rectangles. The easiest method would be to use a decimally divided scale, but it is the one least fitted to bring into relief and fix in the memory their properties. The ratios between the ends and sides expressed numerically are as follows:

>   Root-two .... 1 : 1.4142
>   Root-three .... 1 : 1.732
>   Root-four .... 1 : 2
>   Root-five .... 1 : 2.236
>   Whirling square .... 1 : 1.618

A better way, particularly for the beginner, is to develop the rectangles from the square — the egg from which they are all hatched — by the use of the diagonal, since by these means they are perceivel to be members of an infinite series having common properties.

This is easily accomplished: The diagonal of each succeeding rectangle, beginning with the square, determines the long side of the next. That is to say, the diagonal of the square, revolved downward until it coincides with the base, forms the long side of a root-two rectangle whose short side is the side of the square. The diagonal of this rectangle, similarly revolved down to meet its base, yields the long side of a root-three rectangle, and so on, as shown in the upper figure of Illustration 12. The lower figure shows the method of developing root-rectangles *inside* the square so clearly that it needs no verbal explanation. The root-four rectangle, being a double square, is established by a single semicircular sweep of the compass. There is a method of drawing a root-five rectangle which is only one degree less simple, and yields, at the same time, the whirling-square rectangle. This is shown in Illustration 11. Let it be noted that a whirling-square rectangle plus its reciprocal is a root-five rectangle: that is, a root-five rectangle equals the area of a whirling-square rectangle horizontal plus one perpendicular. A method of forming the root-five and whirling-square rectangles within the square is shown in Illustration 26.

REGULATING LINES

The most interesting thing about the whirling-square rectangle is that the ratio between its end and its side — 1:618 — is the same as that between any two adjoining terms of a converging summation series, so called because each succeeding term of the system is obtained by adding the two preceding terms. This ratio expresses the important fact in the growth of plants known as phyllotaxis, or leaf-distribution. If, therefore, the whirling-square rectangle, which is this ratio in graphic representation, be used as a determining factor in design, an observed law of nature is carried by these means into art.*

Design, in the last analysis, is purely a matter of space-subdivision, and as such is all compounded of mathematical relations. If these relations are *orderly,* based on some law or laws, instead of being merely fortuitous, it makes for beauty — or whatever name one may give to that thing which Leonardo apostrophized as " O marvelous necessity!" Now dynamic symmetry, based on a system of interrelated rectangles possessing amazing properties in common and all referable to a single generic figure, the logarithmic spiral, provides such a needed mathematical *warp* — stretched threads on which it is possible to weave any design whatsoever. This *woof,* or free-spreading pattern, however various and vagarious, will be subtly acted upon thereby: numerical truth will *show through* as visible beauty.

A BAS-RELIEF FROM EGYPT, SHOWING A SQUARE DYNAMICALLY DIVIDED BY A WHIRLING SQUARE (HORIZONTAL) AND A ROOT-FIVE (VERTICAL) RECTANGLE — FROM "DYNAMIC SYMMETRY THE GREEK VASE" BY JAY HAMBIDGE.

14

The square, the first four root-rectangles, the rectangle of the whirling squares, and such others as are formed by a process of addition and

---

* The ratio of the sides of the whirling square rectangle is the same as the proportion called "Divine Intersection" (*sectio divina*) by which the ratio of the shorter part of an intersected line to the longer is the same as the ratio of this longer part to the whole line. The exact numerical value of this proportion is 1.618034. The figures 0.618034 and 1.618034 happen to be the only two values whose product as well as whose difference are equal and amount to unity.

subtraction, together with their reciprocals, their diagonals, the perpendiculars to the diagonals, and the derived subdivisions, constitute a system of *regulating lines,* applicable alike to pictorial, sculptural, or architectural problems. The manner of such application is shown in Mr. Hambidge's books: it is simple, yet infinitely various; precise, and yet elastic.

Illustration 14, from *Dynamic Symmetry: The Greek Vase,* reproduces an Egyptian bas-relief. Fillets at top and bottom define a square: this square is dynamically subdivided by means of a horizontal whirling-square rectangle and a vertical root-five rectangle, established by drawing lines through the intersections of the diagonals of the whirling-square rectangle with their perpendiculars. The web of lines thus formed determine the main elements of the composition. That the use of this order of regulating lines by the Egyptians was a reasoned and a conscious thing, as claimed by Mr. Hambidge, seems indicated in this case by the clear definition given the root-five rectangle by means of the vertical wands, and by the fact that the hands of the two figures are placed exactly at the intersection of the diagonals of the whirling-square rectangle with their perpendiculars, the two points which establish the root-five rectangle and the poles of the two spirals.

In casting about for other illustrations it occurred to me that it would be amusing to try out dynamic symmetry on the work of artists who used it consciously not at all. On the walls of my room are five pictures, selected out of a great number for the reason that they so satisfy my sense of color and design. To what extent, I wondered, would they submit themselves to a geometrical synopsis along the lines of dynamic symmetry?

The three which I selected as most likely to produce interesting results were one of Hokusai's best known and most beautiful color prints, *The Waterfall;* a setting for *The Idle Inn* by Robert Edmund Jones; and Aubrey Beardsley's bitingly satirical black-and-white, *Lady Gold's Escort,* rifled from *The Yellow Book* (Illustrations 15, 16, and 18). Now Hokusai and Beardsley could never have heard of dynamic symmetry, and that Jones had no thought of it when he made this drawing I feel sure.

Is it not remarkable as indicating that " the artist follows the rules without knowing them " that every one of these drawings should prove to be, in its main dimensions, one of the root-rectangles, and that the sub-

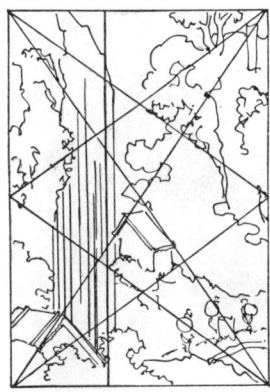

"THE WATERFALL" — A
ROOT-TWO RECTANGLE
THE DIAGONALS WELL
DEFINED BY THE ROOFS
OF THE HOUSES, ETC
ALSO, A VERTICAL
ROOT-FIVE RECTANGLE

17

15

16

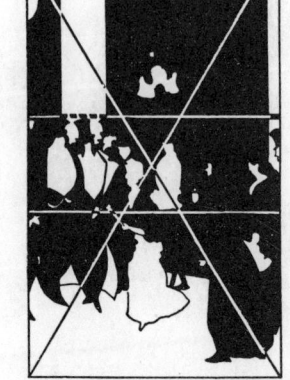

"LADY GOLD'S ESCORT"
WHIRLING SQUARE RECT-
ANGLE WITH REPEATING
SQUARES, THEIR OVERLAP-
PING DEFINED BY THE
HATS, HEADS AND SHIRT-
FRONTS OF THE FIGURES.

20

18

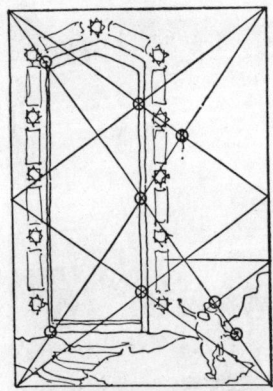

"THE GLITTERING GATE"
A ROOT-TWO RECTANGLE
INTERSECTIONS OF DIAG-
ONALS AND PERPENDICULARS
DETERMINING ELEMENTS
21

"THE IDLE INN" — ROOT-FOUR RECTANGLE WITH
DIAGONALS STRONGLY EMPHASIZED AND FLANKING
MASS ON RIGHT COINCIDENT WITH PERPENDICULARS
19

division of their areas by means of diagonals, perpendiculars, and so forth should yield in every case a clearly traceable relation between this geometrical web and the main lines and masses of the composition?

The Hokusai print is a root-two rectangle with both diagonals fairly well defined, particularly in the lower half of their length by the alignment of the house roofs and the central figure on the bridge — the one bearing a burden. The limiting vertical line of the waterfall defines with fair exactness a root-five rectangle, and the overhanging cliff at the right *echoes* the line of the main diagonal (Illustration 17).

The *Idle Inn* drawing is a double square, hence a root-four rectangle, the diagonal emphasized in the most positive manner by the streaks of light in the sky and the silhouette of gateway and fence. The intersection of the diagonal with its perpendicular at the left of the picture and of the perpendicular with the long side of the rectangle at the right yields verticals which coincide with major elements of the design (Illustration 19).

The Beardsley drawing is a whirling-square rectangle; the square is repeated, top and bottom, and the area included in the overlapping of the two is so clearly defined by the heads and shirt-fronts of the group of Lady Gold's attendant squires that the composition itself gives the clue to this subdivision: all of the interest is concentrated in this area, for it contains the heads and torsos of nine out of the ten figures. Lady Gold's hand and the head of the muff-bearer define the diagonal (Illustration 20).

The fact that these drawings, done by artists who made no use of dynamic symmetry, submit themselves to a dynamically symmetrical synopsis is sure to be interpreted by some readers as discrediting Mr. Hambidge's idea, but to me it seems a confirmation of it. I interpret it as meaning that the æsthetic intuition works *mathematically*, and achieves, by its own subterranean processes, and without the aid of calculation, the desired results. The question then naturally arises: why *have* rules, and what gain is there in knowing them?

To this there is an effective answer suggested by the sister art of music. The natural-born composer will intuitively obey the great generic laws which are at the root of music but he cannot on that account afford to dispense with their formulation as embodied in the science of harmony, because, lacking this knowledge, he would do a great deal of unnecessary fumbling about, and he would fall short of his highest potentiality of self-expression. Now dynamic symmetry bears much the same relation to the arts of space as does the science of harmony to musical composition: On the purely creative side it has only a negative value, being no substitute for inspiration or ideation — out of sows' ears it will make no silk purses. On the technical side, however, it has a very definite value.

Let me attempt to demonstrate this by an example from my own experience. I have a conception of a "glittering gate" inspired by reading Lord Dunsany's one-act play of this title, and I want to put my idea in the form of a drawing. The general image is quite clear in my mind, but this does not tell me just where, within the confines of my parallelogram, the great opening in the wall of heaven would look best, nor what proportions would be most happy. Therefore I call dynamic symmetry to my aid, with the result shown in Illustration 22, in which the position and proportions have been determined by the intersections of diagonals and perpendiculars within a root-two rectangle (Illustration 21). Of the rightness of the space-relations arrived at by these means I leave the reader to judge, but if that judgment be favorable — if the placing and spacing satisfy the eye — there is no doubt that this result is due to the correlating power of *the diagonal*.

The architectural designer should master the principles of dynamic symmetry in the same spirit that a musical composer learns harmony — as a useful and necessary part of his equipment for self-expression. To this end the essentials of the system in condensed and organized form, are contained in the following four pages of diagrams (Illustrations 23, 24, 25, and 26).

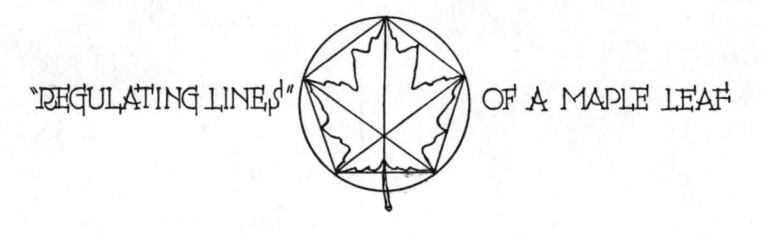

"REGULATING LINES" OF A MAPLE LEAF

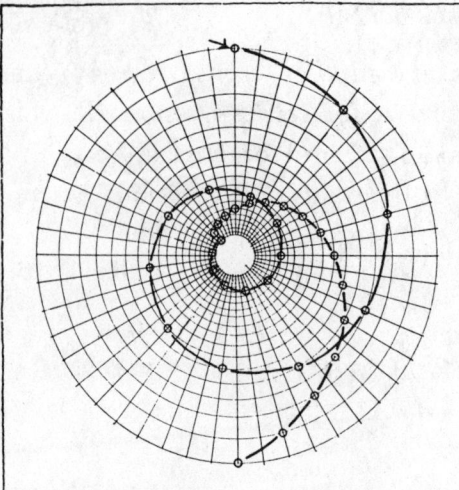

A METHOD FOR LAYING OUT A LOGARITHMIC SPIRAL

DIVIDE A CIRCLE INTO A MESHWORK OF SQUARES FORMED BY CONCENTRIC CIRCLES AND EQUALLY SPACED RADII — ALL LINES DRAWN THROUGH THE INTERSECTIONS WILL BE LOGARITHMIC SPIRALS IF DONE IN SOME CONSTANT MANNER

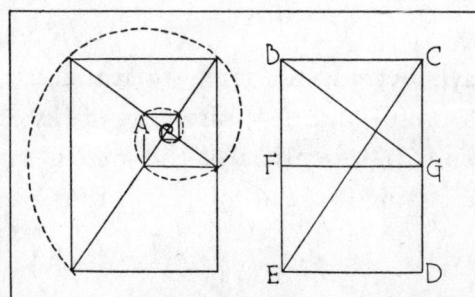

THE FIRST AND MOST FUNDAMENTAL APPLICATION OF THE LOGARITHMIC SPIRAL TO THE ARTS OF DESIGN

THIS CONSISTS OF THE PLACING OF THE ANGULAR SPIRAL WITHIN A RECTANGLE, WHICH MAY BE DONE BY DRAWING A DIAGONAL TO THE RECTANGLE, AND FROM ONE OF THE REMAINING CORNERS A LINE WHICH CUTS THE DIAGONAL AT RIGHT ANGLES, PRODUCED TO THE OPPOSITE SIDE OF THE RECTANGLE. SUCH A LINE (A) IS CALLED A PERPENDICULAR, AND IN ALL CASES IT IS DRAWN FROM A CORNER, AND ESTABLISHES PROPORTION WITHIN A RECTANGLE, AND IS THE DIAGONAL TO THE RECIPROCAL OF THE RECTANGLE — FOR EXAMPLE THE RECTANGLE BCGF IS THE RECIPROCAL OF THE RECTANGLE BCDE

ROOT RECTANGLES — PROPERTIES and FORMATION

THERE IS AN INFINITE SERIES OF RECTANGLES POSSESSING INTERESTING PROPERTIES. FIRST, THEIR SIDES ARE DIVIDED INTO EQUAL PARTS BY THE PERPENDICULAR TO THE DIAGONAL; SECOND, THOUGH THE ENDS AND SIDES ARE INCOMMENSURABLE IN LINE THEY ARE COMMENSURABLE IN SQUARE — OF THESE "ROOT RECTANGLES" ONLY THE FIRST FOUR ARE IMPORTANT TO THE DESIGNER, AND PARTICULARLY THE FIRST AND FOURTH

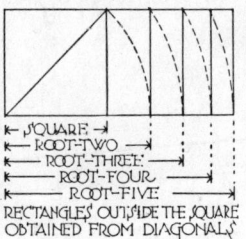

RECTANGLES OUTSIDE THE SQUARE OBTAINED FROM DIAGONALS

THE ROOT RECTANGLES ARE DEVELOPED FROM THE SQUARE, THE "SEED OR ETERNAL ROOT" BY A SIMPLE GEOMETRICAL METHOD

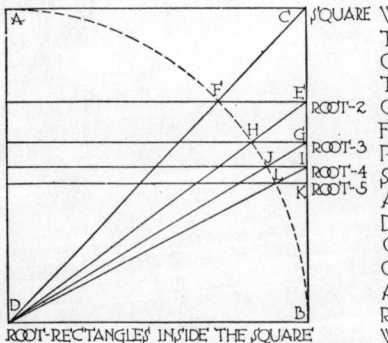

ROOT RECTANGLES INSIDE THE SQUARE

WITHIN THE SQUARE DRAW THE QUADRANT ARC A,B, WITH CENTER D AND RADIUS D.B. THE DIAGONAL OF THE SQUARE CUTS THE QUADRANT ARC AT F. THROUGH F DRAW A LINE PARALLEL TO THE SIDE OF THE SQUARE. THIS LINE DETERMINES A ROOT-TWO RECTANGLE AND D E IS ITS DIAGONAL. A DIAGONAL TO A ROOT-TWO RECTANGLE CUTS THE QUADRANT ARC AT H. G D IS A ROOT-THREE RECTANGLE THE DIAGONAL OF WHICH CUTS THE QUADRANT ARC AT J. D I IS A ROOT-FOUR RECTANGLE AND ITS DIAGONAL CUTS THE QUADRANT ARC AT L. D K IS A ROOT-FIVE RECTANGLE AND SO ON

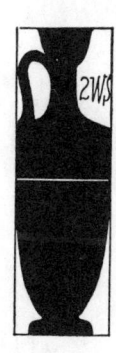

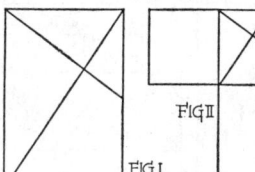

PROPERTIES OF THE ROOT-TWO RECTANGLE

FIG I. √2-RECTANGLE   FIG II. AREA OF SQUARES 1:2

FIGURE I REPRESENTS A ROOT-TWO RECTANGLE — ONE WHEREIN THE PERPENDICULAR TO THE DIAGONAL BISECTS THE LONG SIDE, AND THE END AND SIDE ARE RELATED AS ONE TO THE SQUARE ROOT OF TWO, OR, 1 : 1.4142. A SQUARE CONSTRUCTED ON THE END IS EXACTLY ONE HALF, IN AREA, OF THE SQUARE CONSTRUCTED ON THE SIDE (FIG. II). THUS THOUGH THE END AND SIDE ARE INCOMMENSURABLE IN LINE, THEY ARE COMMENSURABLE IN SQUARE.

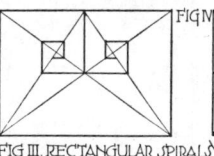

FIG III. RECTANGULAR SPIRALS   FIG IV. SUBDIVISION BY RATIO 2

FIGURE III SHOWS TWO PERPENDICULARS IN THE RECTANGLE, AND RECTANGULAR SPIRALS WRAPPING AROUND TWO POLES OR EYES. IF, AS IN FIG. IV, FOUR PERPENDICULARS ARE DRAWN TO THE TWO DIAGONALS, AND THEN LINES AT RIGHT ANGLES TO THE SIDES AND ENDS THROUGH THE INTERSECTIONS, THE AREA OF THE RECTANGLE WILL BE DIVIDED INTO SIMILAR FIGURES TO THE WHOLE.

IF, INSTEAD OF THE LINES COINCIDING WITH THE SPIRAL WRAPPING (FIG IV), LINES BE DRAWN THROUGH THE EYES, AT RIGHT ANGLES TO THE SIDES AND ENDS, THE RECTANGLE WILL BE DIVIDED INTO SIMILAR SHAPES TO THE WHOLE.

FIG V. SUBDIVISION BY RATIO OF 3

THE ROOT-THREE RECTANGLE

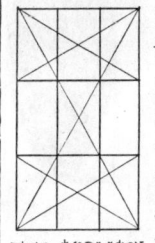

FIG I. SUBDIVISION

IN THE SAME WAY THAT THE ROOT-TWO RECTANGLE IS DEVELOPED FROM A SQUARE (THE DIAGONAL OF THE SQUARE BECOMING THE SIDE OF THE RECTANGLE) THE NEXT, THE ROOT THREE RECTANGLE, IS DEVELOPED FROM THE ROOT TWO, THE DIAGONAL OF THE LATTER DETERMINING THE LONG SIDE OF THE FORMER AS IN FIG II

THE SQUARE ON THE END OF THE ROOT-THREE RECTANGLE IS ONE THIRD THE AREA OF THE SQUARE ON THE SIDE. THE RATIO BETWEEN ITS END AND ITS SIDE IS 1 TO 1.732, OR THE SQUARE ROOT OF 3.

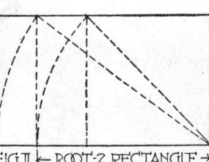

FIG II. ROOT-2 RECTANGLE / ROOT-3 RECTANGLE. FORMATION OF √3 RECTANGLE

THIS RECTANGLE IS DIVIDED INTO THREE EQUAL PARTS BY HORIZONTAL LINES DRAWN THROUGH THE POINTS OF INTERSECTION OF THE PERPENDICULARS AND THE SIDES. IT DIVIDES ITSELF INTO SIMILAR SHAPES TO THE WHOLE WITH A RATIO OF 3 (FIG. I). LINES THROUGH THE EYES OF THE SPIRAL DIVIDE THE RECTANGLE INTO 4 EQUAL PARTS.

THE ROOT-FOUR RECTANGLE

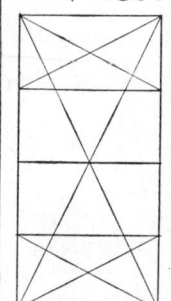

FIG I. DIVISION INTO 4

THE AREA OF THE SQUARE ON THE END OF A ROOT-FOUR RECTANGLE IS ONE FOURTH THE AREA OF THE SQUARE ON THE SIDE. THE RATIO BETWEEN ITS END AND ITS SIDE IS AS 1 TO 2, OR UNITY TO THE SQUARE ROOT OF FOUR.

IT HAS PROPERTIES SIMILAR TO THOSE OF A ROOT-TWO OR A ROOT-THREE RECTANGLE EXCEPT THAT IT DIVIDES ITSELF INTO SIMILAR SHAPES BY A RATIO OF 4.

ITS SIDE IS DIVIDED INTO FOUR EQUAL PARTS BY A PERPENDICULAR. LINES DRAWN THROUGH THE EYES OF THE SPIRALS DIVIDE ITS AREA AS SHOWN IN FIG. III.

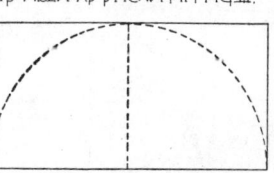

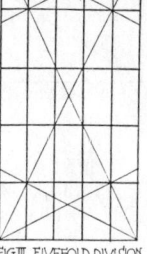

FIG II. FORMATION FROM RADIUS OF CIRCLE   FIG III. FIVEFOLD DIVISION

THE ROOT-FIVE RECTANGLE

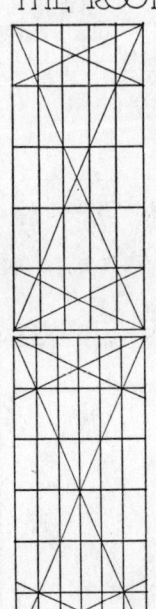

THE AREA OF THE SQUARE ON THE END OF A ROOT-FIVE RECTANGLE IS ONE FIFTH OF THE AREA OF THE SQUARE ON THE SIDE. THE RATIO BETWEEN ITS END AND ITS SIDE IS AS 1 TO 2.236, OR UNITY TO THE SQUARE ROOT OF FIVE.

THE PROPERTIES OF THE ROOT-FIVE RECTANGLE ARE SIMILAR TO THE OTHERS DESCRIBED EXCEPT THAT IT DIVIDES ITSELF INTO RECTANGLES SIMILAR TO THE WHOLE WITH RATIOS OF FIVE AND SIX.

DRAW A SQUARE AND BISECT ONE SIDE AT A WITH RADIUS A.B DESCRIBE SEMI-CIRCLE CBFD DE IS A ROOT-FIVE RECTANGLE.

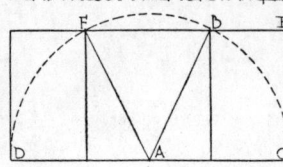

THE WHIRLING SQUARE RECTANGLE AND THE ROOT-FIVE RECTANGLE INSCRIBED WITHIN THE SQUARE

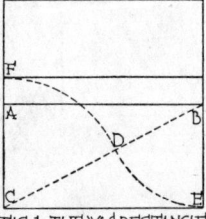

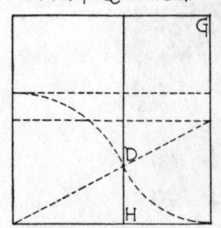

FIG 1. THE W.S RECTANGLE   FIG 2. THE √5 RECTANGLE

THE WHIRLING SQUARE RECTANGLE AND THE ROOT FIVE RECTANGLE ARE PLACED WITHIN THE SQUARE ACCORDING TO THE FOLLOWING METHOD

THE SQUARE IS FIRST BISECTED BY THE LINE A.B, TO OBTAIN A ROOT-FOUR RECTANGLE, OR TWO SQUARES. FROM THE DIAGONAL OF THIS RECTANGLE (C.B). SUBTRACT UNITY, OR B.E TO DETERMINE THE POINT D C.D THEN ESTABLISHES THE SIDE OF THE WHIRLING SQUARE RECTANGLE F.E (FIG 1)

A LINE DRAWN THROUGH THE POINT D PARALLEL TO A SIDE OF THE SQUARE DETERMINES THE ROOT-FIVE RECTANGLE G. H (FIG 2)

THE RECTANGLE OF THE WHIRLING SQUARES

WHAT IS KNOWN AS "NORMAL PHYLLOTAXIS," OR LEAF DISTRIBUTION IN PLANTS IS REPRESENTED BY A CURIOUS SYSTEM OF NUMBERS WHICH ARE KNOWN AS A SUMMATION SERIES, SO CALLED BECAUSE THE SUCCEEDING TERMS, BEGINNING WITH THE LOWEST WHOLE NUMBER ARE OBTAINED BY ADDING TOGETHER THE TWO PRECEDING TERMS. THUS: 1, 2, 3, 5, 8, 13, 21, 34, 55, 89, 144, ETC.

THIS PRODUCES A CERTAIN RATIO, 1.618, WHICH IS OBTAINED BY DIVIDING ANY ONE TERM OF THE SUMMATION SERIES BY ITS PREDECESSOR.

THIS RATIO OF 1.618 IS USED WITH UNITY TO FORM A RECTANGLE WHICH IS DIVIDED BY A DIAGONAL AND A PERPENDICULAR TO THE DIAGONAL, AS IN ROOT RECTANGLES (FIG 1). B.D IS A SQUARE; B.C. IS THE LINE WHICH CREATES SIMILAR FIGURES TO THE WHOLE. WE MAY CALL THIS "THE RECTANGLE OF THE WHIRLING SQUARES" BECAUSE ITS CONTINUED RECIPROCALS CUT OFF SQUARES 1,2,3,4,5, ETC (FIG 2), ARE SQUARES WHIRLING AROUND THE POLE O.

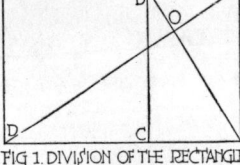

FIG 1. DIVISION OF THE RECTANGLE

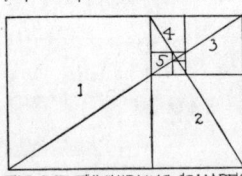

FIG 2 THE WHIRLING SQUARES

THE AREA OF A ROOT-FIVE RECTANGLE IS EQUAL TO THE AREA OF A WHIRLING SQUARE RECTANGLE PLUS ITS RECIPROCAL, I.E., IT EQUALS ONE WHIRLING SQUARE RECTANGLE HORIZONTAL PLUS ONE PERPENDICULAR FOR THE RATIO 1.618, FROM 2.236, OR THE SQUARE ROOT OF 5. LEAVES .618.

FIG 3. SHOWING THE RELATION BETWEEN A ROOT-5 AND A WHIRLING SQUARE RECTANGLE

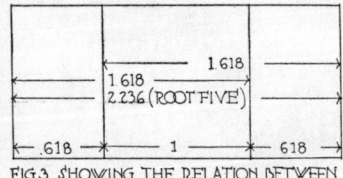

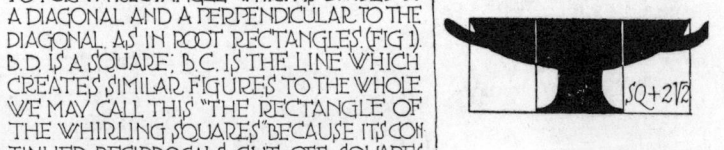

√5

SQ + 2√2

W.S.

"THE APPLICATION OF AREAS" ROOT-2 RECTANGLE & SQUARE

FIG 1. APPLICATION OF SQUARE ON END OF √2 RECTANGLE TO AREA

FIG 2. APPLICATION OF TWO OVERLAPPING SQUARES TO AREA

RECTANGULAR AREAS MAY BE EXHAUSTED BY THE APPLICATION OF OTHER AREAS, AND THE RESULTANT PROPORTIONAL PARTS USED AS ELEMENTS OF DESIGN THUS:

THE SQUARE ON THE END OF A ROOT-TWO RECTANGLE, APPLIED TO ITS AREA, "FALLS SHORT," AND THE PART LEFT OVER IS COMPOSED OF A SQUARE AND A ROOT-TWO RECTANGLE (FIG 1). IF THE SAME SQUARE BE APPLIED TO THE OTHER END, SO AS TO OVERLAP THE FIRST SQUARE, THE AREA IS DIVIDED INTO THREE SQUARES AND THREE ROOT-TWO RECTANGLES (FIG 2). IF THE SQUARE ON THE SIDE OF A ROOT-TWO RECTANGLE BE APPLIED, THE "EXCESS" IS TWO SQUARES AND ONE ROOT-TWO RECTANGLE

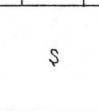

SQUARE ON SIDE √2 □

OTHER WHIRLING SQUARE & ROOT-FIVE RECTANGLES WITHIN A SQUARE

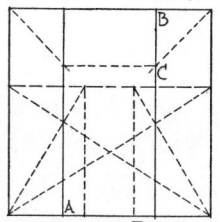

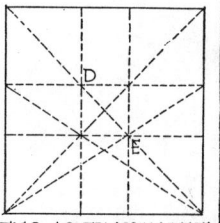

FIG 1. UPRIGHT √5 RECTANGLE

FIG 2. 4-OVERLAPPING W.S. R'S

IN A WHIRLING SQUARE RECTANGLE INSCRIBED IN A SQUARE, IF LINES BE DRAWN THROUGH THE EYES AND PRODUCED TO THE OPPOSITE SIDE OF THE SQUARE, A ROOT-FIVE RECTANGLE IS CONSTRUCTED IN THE CENTER OF THE SQUARE—A,B, FIG. 1. AND IF THESE LINES BE MADE TO TERMINATE AT THEIR INTERSECTION WITH THE DIAGONALS OF THE SQUARE, THE WHIRLING SQUARE RECTANGLE A,C RESULTS

WHEN, AS IN FIG. 2, A WHIRLING SQUARE RECTANGLE IS IN A SQUARE, AND THE SIDES OF THE SMALL CENTRAL SQUARE D,E ARE PRODUCED TO THE SIDES OF THE LARGE SQUARE THE MAJOR SQUARE BECOMES A NEST OF SQUARES AND WHIRLING SQUARE RECTANGLES.

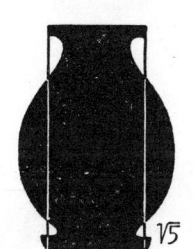

W.S.   √4   √5

26

SINBAD ASCENDS THE ISOMETRIC STAIRS

VI

ISOMETRIC PERSPECTIVE

ARCHITECTURE, having to do pre-eminently with solids, the architectural designer should accustom himself to think always in terms of three dimensions rather than of two. And because perspective is the science of representing solids in plane projection — three dimensions through the mediumship of two — it should form part of his equipment no less than the knowledge and employment of regulating lines.

Many palpable faults and shortcomings of contemporary architectural practice can be traced to the all but universal custom of designing in elevation instead of in perspective — to *the lack of three-dimensional visualization,* a power which the practice of perspective brings. Through lack of mastery of the method, time pressure, or sheer indolence, it too often happens that a building is developed two-dimensionally and the task of making a perspective of it delegated to some subordinate or to a specialist, after the designing is done instead of while still in process; and this with an eye only on its selling value, so that the professional renderer, or perspective expert, has come to stand in much the same relation to the designer as does the "song plugger" employed by music houses to the composer of songs.

The advantage of a more liberal use of perspective than is common among architects generally was brought home to me only after I had entered the field of theatrical production. For a stage scene does not lend itself as readily as does a building to representation by means of plan, elevation, and section; it can be adequately represented only in model form. Models, however, are difficult to make, cumbersome, and expensive; above all, they take time, and in the theater, of all places, everything must be done at top speed. Now the perspective drawing of a scene, though not fulfilling all the uses of a model, can sometimes be made to serve as its substitute. It possesses this advantage over a model, that human figures and stage properties are so easily represented — an important consideration when it is realized that a scene exists solely for the actors, that it is not so much a matter of background as of *environment,* the properties being often of more importance than the backdrop. Under the stimulus of necessity I acquired what might be called the perspective habit, and I am sure it would be an excellent thing if architects were forced from the very start to dramatize their conceptions in this way rather than by the plan-and-elevation method.

But the ordinary type of perspective drawing is both difficult and awkward to make and sometimes involves problems in projection not easily solved. This is the chief reason why the art is not more universally practiced. There is, however, a type of perspective, known as *isometric,* which is rapid, easy, direct; shows things truly and clearly, is " of equal measure " in all three dimensions, and requires no other paraphernalia than working drawings require.

Isometric perspective might be a great aid to the architectural designer — as it was to me in my theatrical work — first, as an easily achieved projection of the mental image, conveying the sense of three-dimensionality without going through the tedious process of point perspective; second, as an interpreter of working drawings to the artisan, an isometric drawing being a *realistic* working drawing — plan, elevation, and section all in one; and, third, because of its being true to scale in all three dimensions it becomes in some cases a more clear and effective working drawing than any other kind.

For purposes of comparison there are shown in Illustration 27 three different methods of representing the same architectural subject — a stairway and an arch in a wall — in plane projection. A is an isometric drawing, the advantages of which are under discussion; B is a pictorial, or vanishing-point perspective; C shows the subject in plan and elevation — that is, in ordinary working-drawing form. A combines the advantages of B and C in that it is sufficiently realistic to be understood at a glance, which is true of B but not of C, and A is true to measurement along the lines of its three perpendiculars, which is true of C but not of B.

Aerial photography, which shows things as they appear from high up and far away — in bird's-eye view — is making this aspect of the world increasingly familiar. When in contact with the earth, one's vision is limited: near objects loom large, concealing those more remote. But as one rises above the earth, that which had been *behind* appears as *beyond;* and things are seen more nearly in their true relations — the picture, without ceasing to be a picture, takes on some of the characteristics of *a map*.

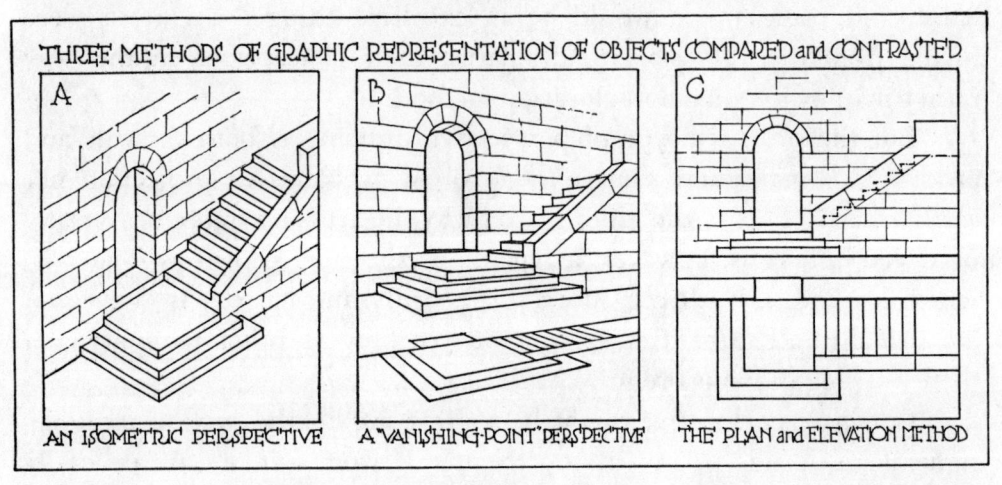

THREE METHODS OF GRAPHIC REPRESENTATION OF OBJECTS COMPARED and CONTRASTED

A — AN ISOMETRIC PERSPECTIVE   B — A "VANISHING-POINT" PERSPECTIVE   C — THE PLAN and ELEVATION METHOD

27

Now an isometric perspective is curiously like an airplane view in that the vanishing-point is far removed — is at infinity, in point of fact — and consequently such a perspective, though itself a distorted image, is free from that order of diminishment and distortion to which ordinary

ISOMETRIC PERSPECTIVE

perspective is subject, for that aims to reproduce the *optical image* in which the size of objects diminishes in proportion to their distance away, and parallel lines converge, which, though true to appearance, is contrary to fact. Isometric perspective, on the other hand, less faithful to appear-

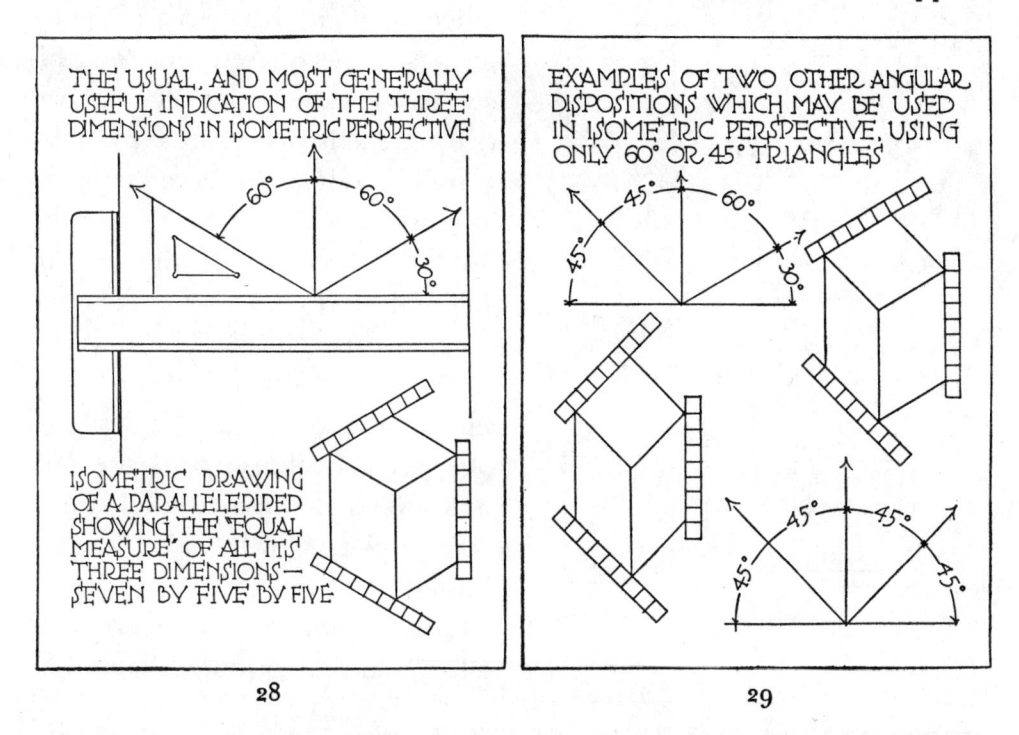

28

29

ance, is more faithful to fact; it shows things more nearly as they are *known to the mind:* Parallel lines are *really* parallel; there is no far and no near, the size of everything remains constant because all things are represented as being the same distance away and the eye of the spectator everywhere at once. When we imagine a thing, or strive to visualize it in the mind or memory, we do it in this way, without the distortions of ordinary perspective. Isometric perspective is therefore more intellectual, more archetypal, it more truly renders *the mental image* — the thing seen by the mind's eye.

The isometric method is so simple that it scarcely needs verbal explanation, which is perhaps the reason that I have found so little written about it. There are no vanishing-points and consequently no diminishments; a thing does not change its size or dimensions by reason of position or distance, because the vanishing-points are at an infinite distance and the eye of the observer at all places at once. To anyone at all skilled in point perspective isometric perspective presents no difficulties, and even without that knowledge the method should be clear by a careful study of the accompanying diagrams. What it amounts to is the correlation in a single drawing of plan and elevations, but in a somewhat distorted form. The drawing will be true to scale on all three perpendiculars, but right angles will have become obtuse or acute and circles (except those parallel to the picture plane) will have become ellipses, just as in point perspective.

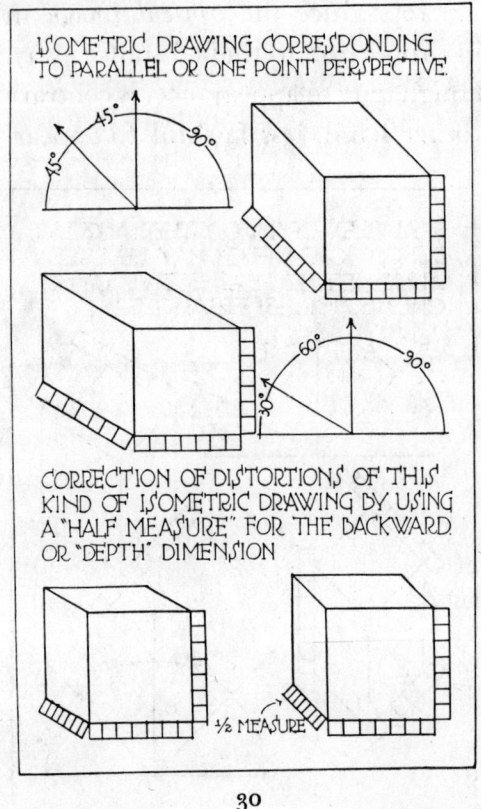

Illustrations 28, 29, 30, and 31 yield the necessary initial data. The first thing to establish is the three perpendiculars. The line representing *height* will invariably be vertical, and the other two — length and breadth

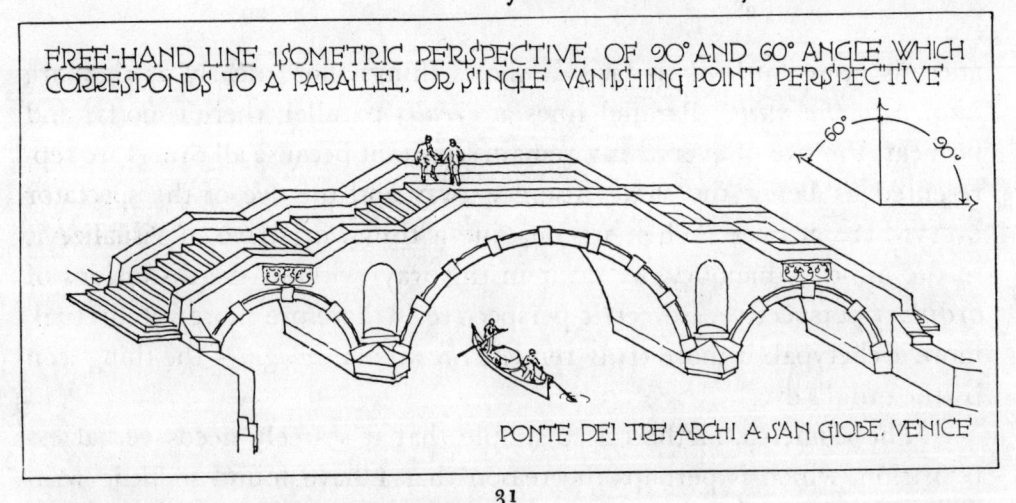

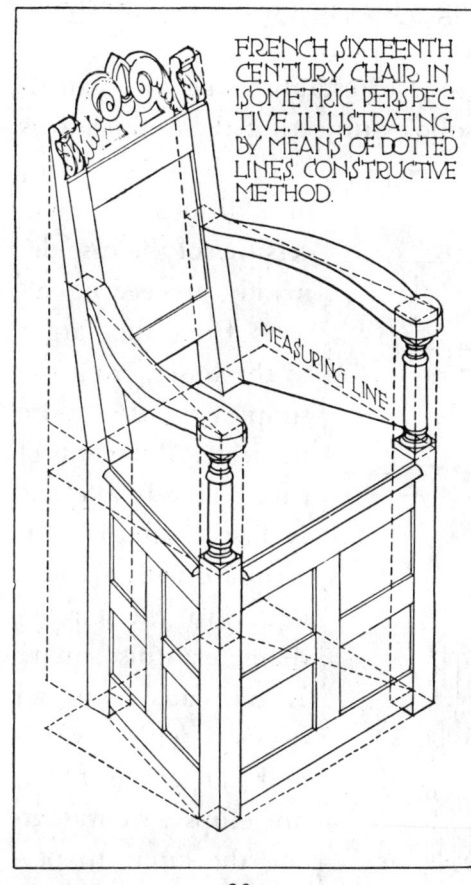

ISOMETRIC PERSPECTIVE

— will be expressed by the two sides of an angle, chosen arbitrarily, ranging from a minimum of ninety to a maximum of one hundred and fifty degrees.

Because the triangles in common use by draughtsmen are of "thirty-sixty" and forty five degrees, the angles usually selected are such as can be worked with these two triangles in conjunction with a T-square. The angles shown in Illustrations 28 and 30 are the ones most commonly employed, but the two others shown in Illustration 29 are useful for special purposes, where it is desired to make the *plan* clear and prominent.

33 — FRENCH SIXTEENTH CENTURY CHAIR IN ISOMETRIC PERSPECTIVE, ILLUSTRATING, BY MEANS OF DOTTED LINES, CONSTRUCTIVE METHOD.

32 — METHOD OF LAYING OUT CIRCLES AND CIRCULAR CURVES

Having established the three perpendiculars, represented by a vertical and the two lines subtending the chosen angle, and corresponding to the dimensions of height, length, and breadth, each becomes a measuring line upon which and by means of which the various elements of a design may be plotted to scale. Herein lies the great advantage of the isometric method, both for simplicity in making and for convenience in a reading: the drawing is to scale on all perpendiculars — of " equal measure," as the name itself implies.

The approved method of procedure is to establish first the plan in perspective, then the main rectilinear solids, subjecting these afterwards to such subdivisions or additions as the necessities of the case demand, proceeding always from the larger to the lesser, from the simple to the more intricate. Pursuant of this method, a circle is first established as a square with a width equal to the circle's diameter; this square is translated into an octagon, within which and tangential to it, an ellipse, representing the circle in perspective, can easily be drawn free-hand (Illustration 32). In Illustration 33, representing a chair in isometric perspective, the dotted lines indicate the preliminary construction and measuring lines. Confusion is avoided by always beginning with the perspective *plan*, and building upward from that into the vertical dimension.

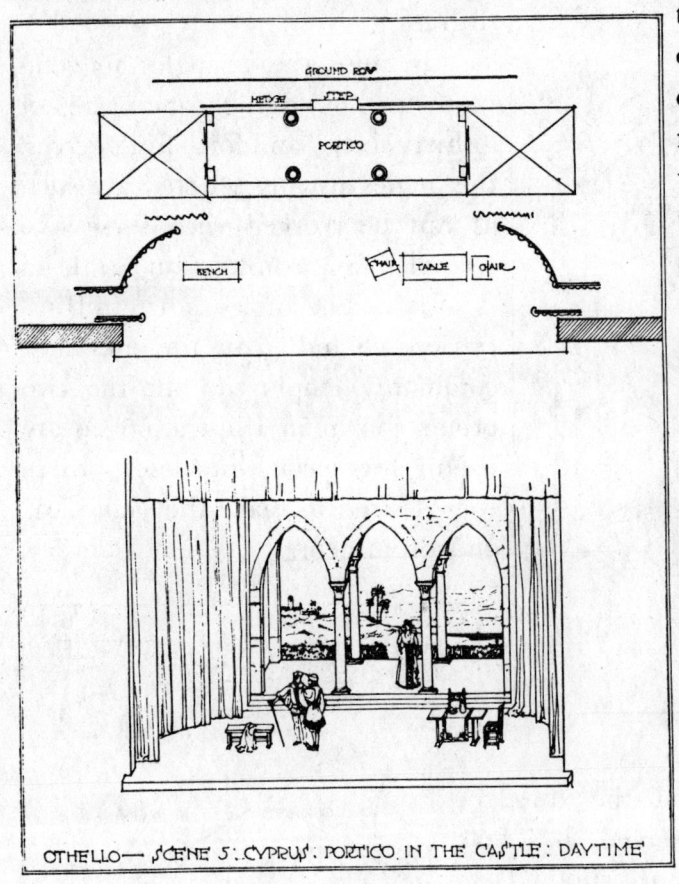

The one-hundred-and-thirty-five-degree and the one-hundred-and-fifty-degree isometric perspectives (Illustrations 30 and 31) correspond to the single-vanishing-point, or parallel perspective, so called. This type of isometric drawing is most happily and easily achieved for the reason that it involves only the adding of the third or depth dimension to a straight

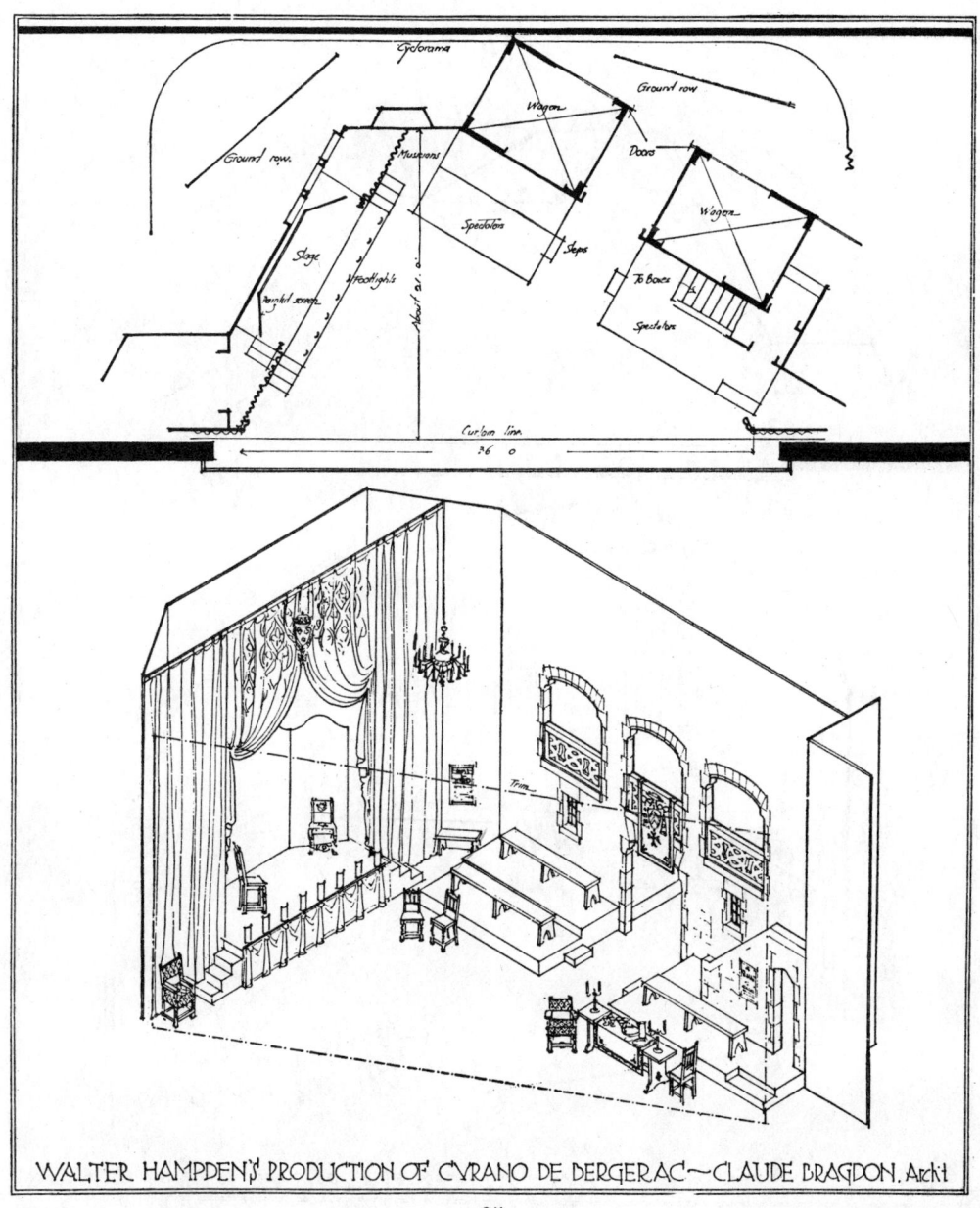

ISOMETRIC PERSPECTIVE

WALTER HAMPDEN'S PRODUCTION OF CYRANO DE BERGERAC — CLAUDE BRAGDON, Arch't

35

elevation. The objection to it dwells in the fact that this third dimension, if " equal measure " is adhered to, appears excessive, and the distortion consequently extreme. To overcome this I conceived the idea of making all measurements on the retreating perpendicular (the depth

66   THE FROZEN FOUNTAIN

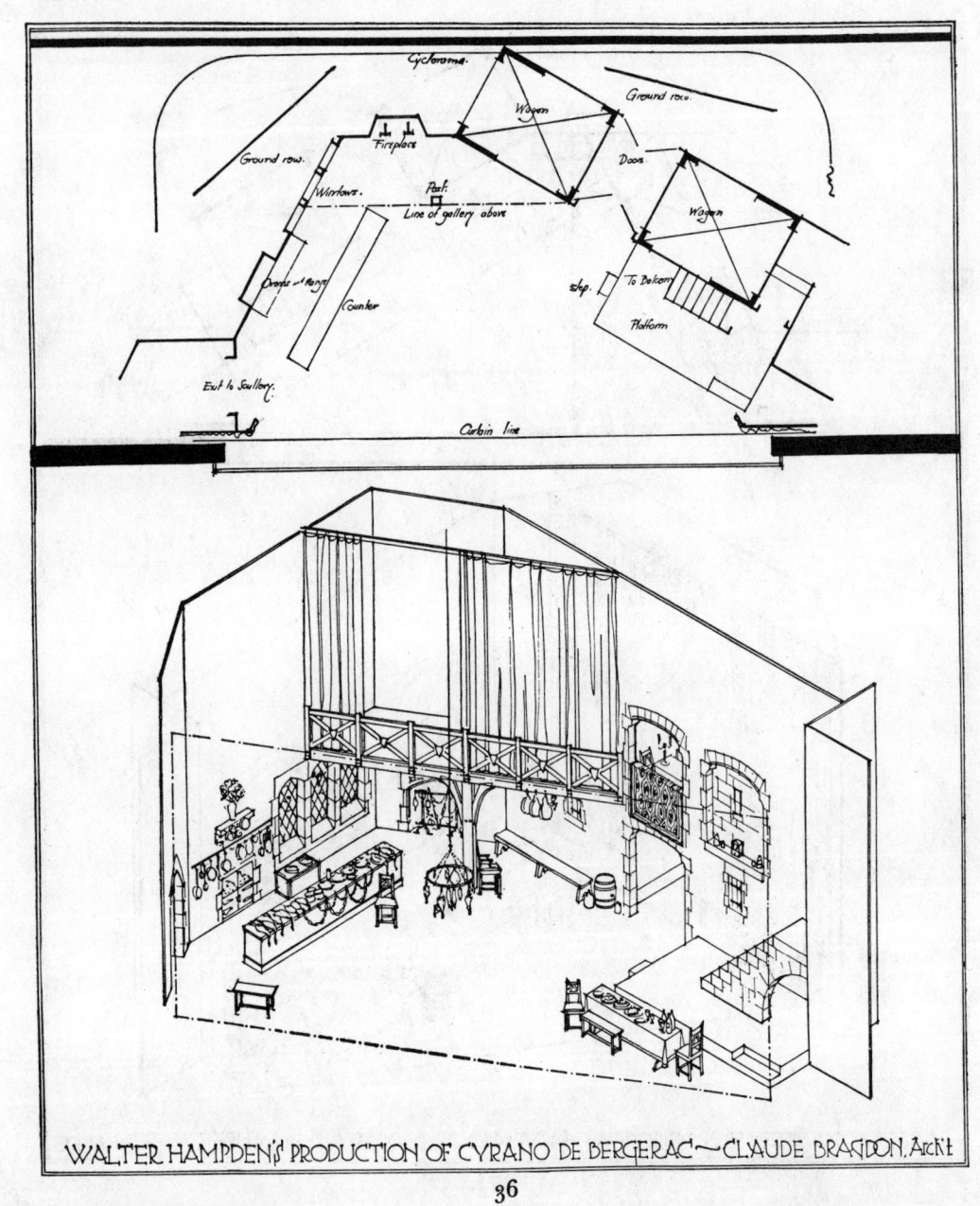

WALTER HAMPDEN'S PRODUCTION OF CYRANO DE BERGERAC — CLAUDE BRAGDON, Arch't

36

dimension) *one half* of what, according to the isometric rule, they should be, as shown in the lower diagram of Illustration 30. Presentations of objects made according to this rule closely approximate true optical perspectives, while the labor is much less. I found this compromise extremely

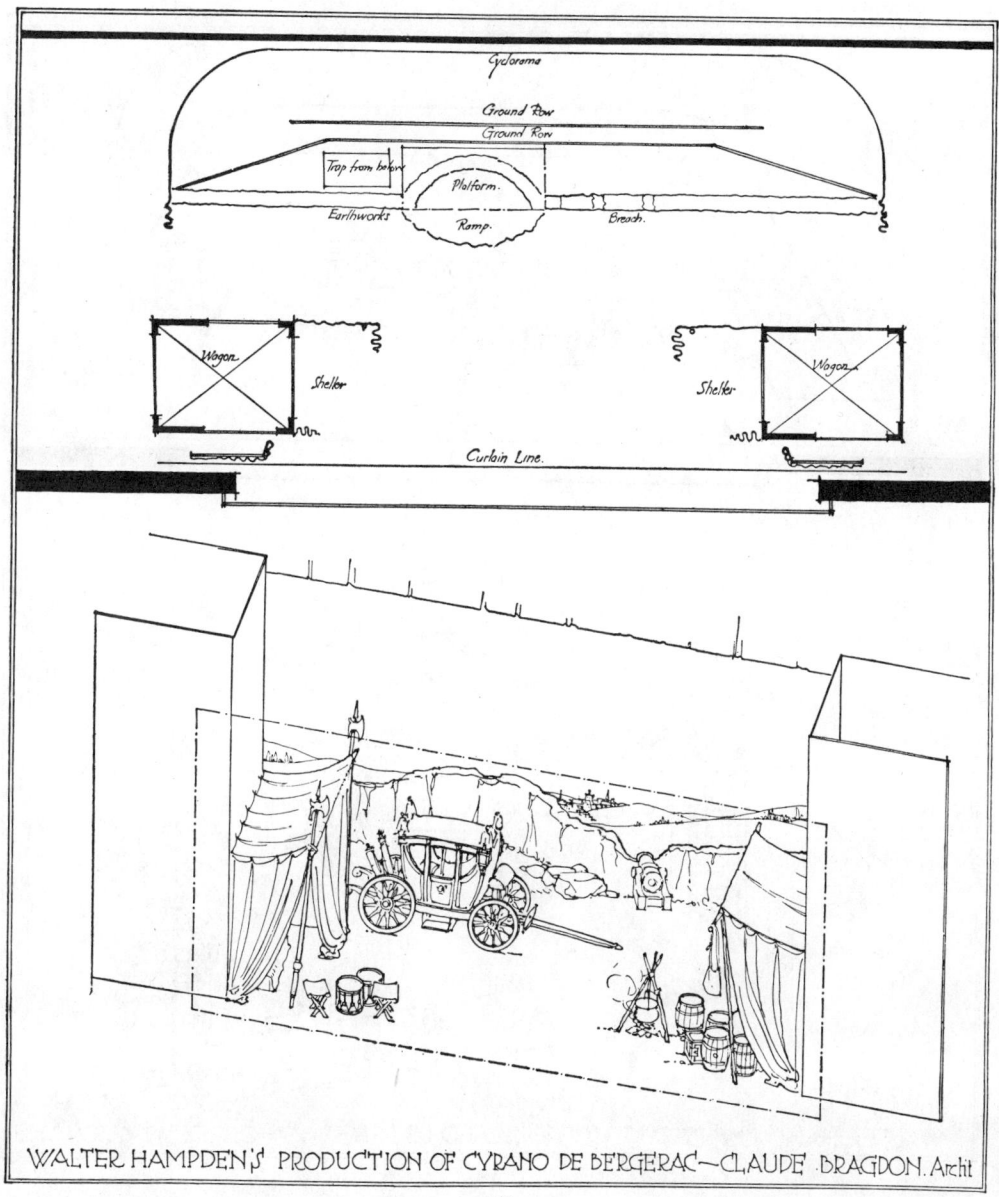

ISOMETRIC PERSPECTIVE

WALTER HAMPDEN'S PRODUCTION OF CYRANO DE BERGERAC—CLAUDE BRAGDON, Archt

37

useful in my work in the theater, for by these means I was able to make a wholly intelligible and quite realistic picture of a stage-setting with scarcely more labor than goes to the making of a straight elevation. Illustration 34 shows a scene in Walter Hampden's production of *Othello*

68 THE FROZEN FOUNTAIN

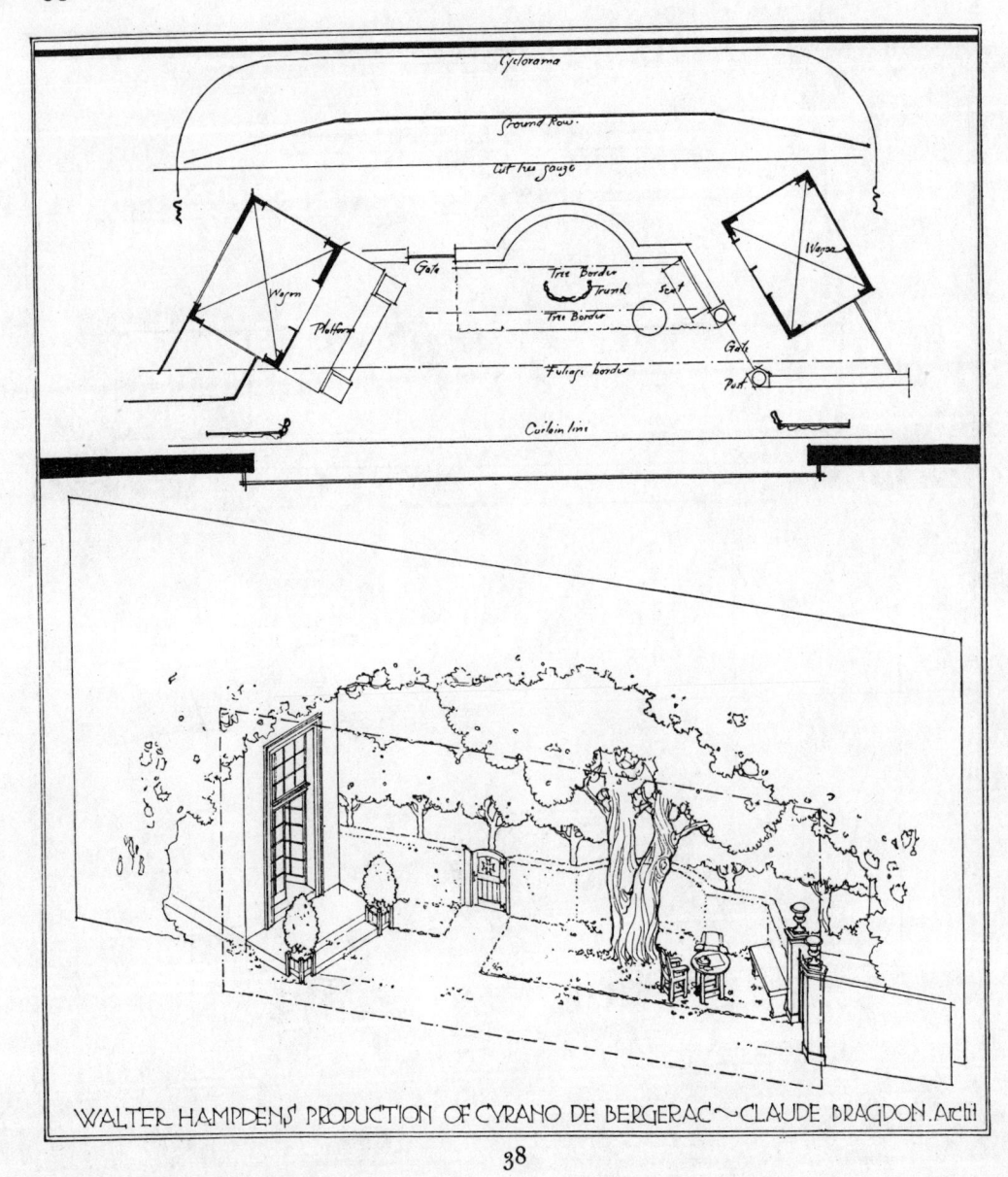

WALTER HAMPDEN'S PRODUCTION OF CYRANO DE BERGERAC ~ CLAUDE BRAGDON, Archt

38

made according to this method, as is also the "Geometrical Garden" which heads the penultimate chapter of this book.

Illustrations 35 to 38, made for Walter Hampden's *Cyrano de Bergerac* production, exemplify some of the higher reaches of the art of isometric perspective, and I would call particular attention to Illustration

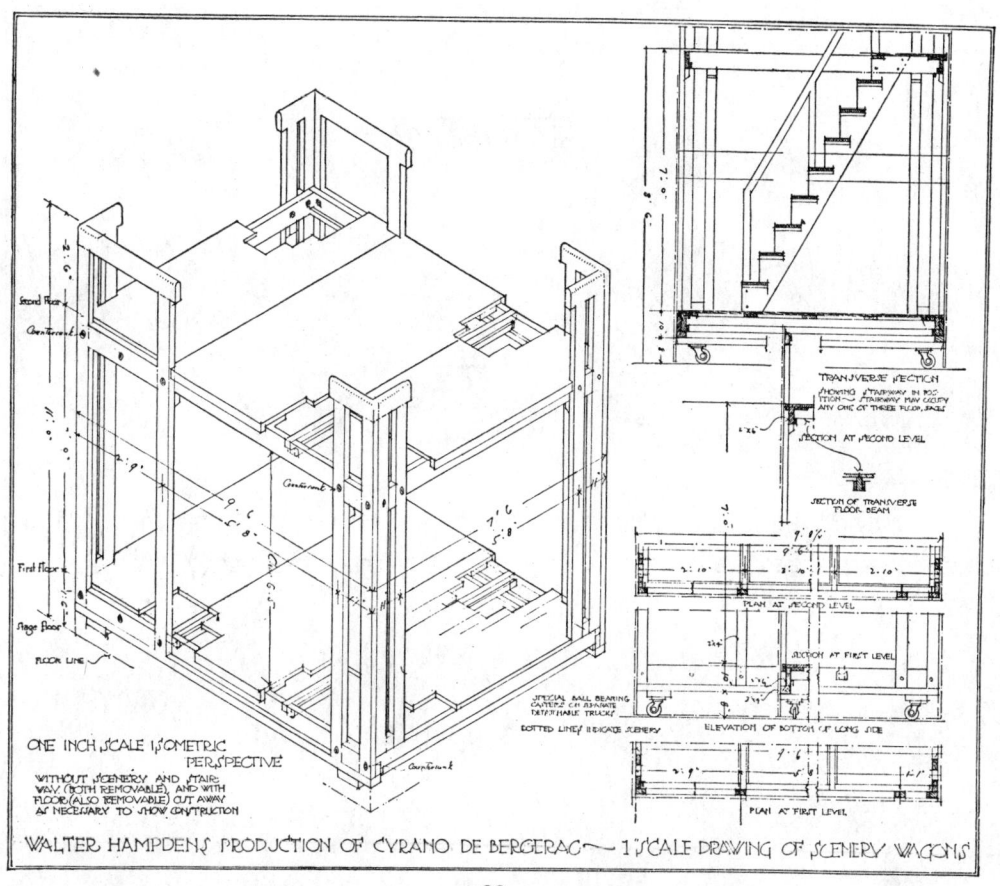

ISOMETRIC PERSPECTIVE

WALTER HAMPDEN'S PRODUCTION OF CYRANO DE BERGERAC — 1½" SCALE DRAWING OF SCENERY WAGONS

39

39 because it so well shows forth the value of isometric perspective as a *correlator* of plan, elevation, and section, making the whole intelligible at a glance.

With the aid of this exposition and these examples anyone, with a little practice, should be able to master this useful and amusing art.

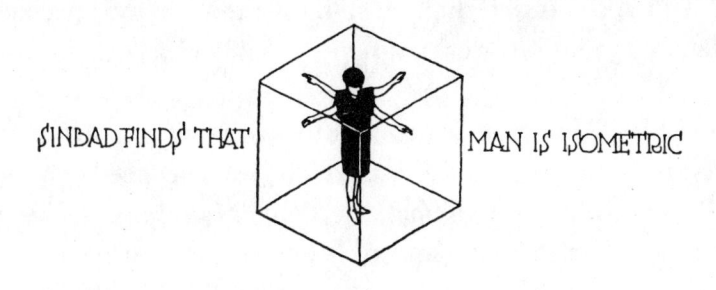

SINBAD FINDS THAT   MAN IS ISOMETRIC

SINBAD [THE ARTIST] IN THE VALLEY OF DIAMONDS [GEOMETRY]

VII
ORNAMENT

ECONOMIC and structural necessity are at last driving us toward the development of an architecture the forms of which will be determined by their functions, as in the case of a machine. And because it is the machine ideal which avowedly, according to its own high priests, inspires this architecture, everything not directly contributory to some kind of *usefulness* is — theoretically at least — tabu. For this reason an outstanding characteristic of the best of the new architecture is the general absence of ornament, for ornament serves no useful practical purpose other than to delight the eye, and a science which has electrocuted Santa Claus concerns itself with other things than delight.

The machine ideal applied to architecture, save in its most utilitarian aspects, is, however, a false one, or at least it needs to be supplemented by something else to make it true. *Man cannot live by bread alone!* He requires also that wine of life which is beauty — a beauty be-

ORNAMENT

yond mere "structural expressiveness." Our age requires, no less than antecedent ages, *an ornamental mode.*

Ornament springs from an impulse no less natural and primitive than singing and dancing. It may even be the same impulse, for is not or-

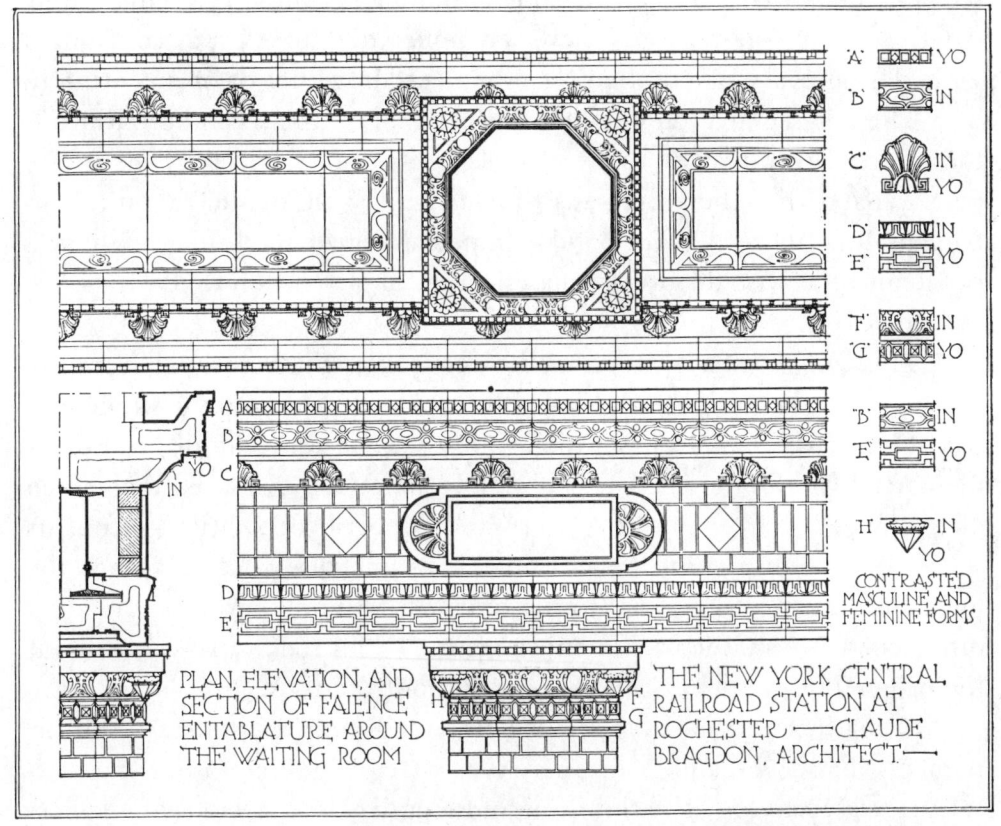

PLAN, ELEVATION, AND SECTION OF FAIENCE ENTABLATURE AROUND THE WAITING ROOM — THE NEW YORK CENTRAL RAILROAD STATION AT ROCHESTER — CLAUDE BRAGDON, ARCHITECT — CONTRASTED MASCULINE AND FEMININE FORMS

40

nament an arrested song, a frozen dance? At any rate the desire for decoration is as primitive and deep-seated, arising from a psychological rather than from a physical necessity — and this is the reason why ornament has ever been and must ever be a mirror of the individual and racial consciousness. The ornament in use today, whether derived or invented, reveals that consciousness to be afflicted by æsthetic sterility — so in its untruth there is truth. There is need of an ornamental mode which shall be eloquent of our *uniqueness*, drawn from the same source from which our power is drawn and in which our interest is centered.

The realization of this need dawned on me first some twenty years ago, when I was called upon to design a railway station for my native city of Rochester, New York. Though I had never been averse to dipping into the dust-bin of *Meyer's Handbook of Ornament,* in this case it seemed imperative that no ornament should be employed which antedated steam transportation. There was none: therefore I was confronted with the necessity of eliminating ornament altogether or of inventing it.

The first seemed too stark an alternative, and the second too difficult for a talent atrophied by that order of parasitism practiced by me in the past. What I did, therefore, was to deal with some of the canonical ornamental motifs with a free hand — much as a jazz-band leader might syncopate or otherwise distort the masterpieces of Beethoven or Bach (Illustration 40).

This compromise, though moderately successful, was so far from satisfying that I thereafter undertook a searching inquiry into the whole subject. One of the first things which impressed me was that all good ornament readily submits itself to a simple geometrical synopsis; that much of it, indeed — like Gothic tracery and Moorish decoration — consists solely of the combination, repetition, or symmetrical assemblage of the most elementary geometrical forms, and that all floral and free-spreading ornament has a mathematical substructure — the rock can exist without the lichen, but the lichen cannot exist without the rock.

In mathematics, then, I seemed to have found the source of all ornament whatsoever, and it was there that I decided to plant my metaphysical spade. Moreover, it is the thing most native to the modern temper: ours is pre-eminently the age of mathematics; it is the one subject that is universally taught; it has given us our control of natural forces; it is the magician's wand without which our workers of magic, be they bankers, engineers, physicists, inventors, could not perform their tricks. Of course this is nothing new: mathematics has long been made to serve man's uses, but never so universally or so successfully as now, threatening to swallow all other knowledges as fast as they assume organized form. Moreover, since the advent of non-Euclidian geometry the field of mathematics has been enlarged, enriched, and, by reason of the theory of relativity, popularized: space-time, curved space, the fourth dimension having become catchwords. In brief, the modern mind is as definitely centered on invention and discovery, of which mathematics is the guiding light, as ever the mediæval mind was centered on Christ, the Virgin, the disciples, and the saints; and just as the cathedrals were decorated with their images, by a parity of reasoning mathematics should be made to furnish forth an ornamental mode for the modern world.

Such was my conclusion, shared, I found afterwards, by Ruskin, who said: " I believe the only manner of rich ornament that is open to us is in geometrical color mosaic, and that much might result from taking up that mode of design." But my position was not unlike that of Watts, who, having noted that the expansive force of steam was sufficient to blow the iron cover off a tea-kettle, had not yet devised a way whereby it could be made to run an engine. My idea was sufficiently sound, but how could it be developed practically?

Keats' dictum, " Beauty is Truth; Truth, Beauty," gave me the clue. Because mathematical truth is absolute within its own limits I had only to discover some method of translation of this *truth-to-the-mind* into *beauty-to-the-eye*. In the course of time I discovered several. These I have described in *Projective Ornament* and, as new possibilities unfolded, in certain essays in *Architecture and Democracy* and *The New Image*. But I now feel that my explanations were unclear and my illustrations not sufficiently convincing, and that the whole matter should be formulated anew. I hope that the already initiated reader will bear with me, therefore, if I repeat myself, on the assurance that " from this time forth I never will speak word."

SINBAD WATCHING INSOMNIUS, THE WHITE KNIGHT, TRACE THE KNIGHT'S TOUR IN CHESS

MAGIC LINES IN MAGIC SQUARES

The three mathematical sources from which I was able to derive ornament were magic paths in magic squares, the Platonic solids, and the diagrammatic representations of the regular hypersolids of four-dimensional space. My first experiments were with magic squares because they constitute such a conspicuous instance of the intrinsic harmony of number — of mathematical truth.

A magic square is a numerical acrostic; a progression of numbers (usually arithmetical) arranged in square form in such a manner that those in each band, whether horizontal, vertical or diagonal shall always form the same sum. Every magic square contains a magic path, discoverable by tracing the numbers in their original and natural sequence from cell to cell and back again to the initial number. This is called *the magic line*. Such a line makes, of necessity, a pattern, interesting always and sometimes beautiful as well. Here is the raw material of ornament: in this way the chasm between mathematical truth and visible beauty may be bridged. It remains only to intensify and utilize this beauty — to deal with the magic line in such a way as to subserve æsthetic ends.

I began with the simplest of all magic squares, that of 3 x 3, consist-

ONE METHOD OF FORMING ODD-NUMBER SQUARES

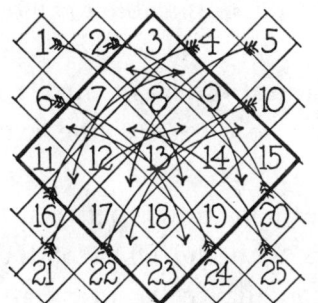

3	16	9	22	15
20	8	21	14	2
7	25	13	1	19
24	12	5	18	6
11	4	17	10	23

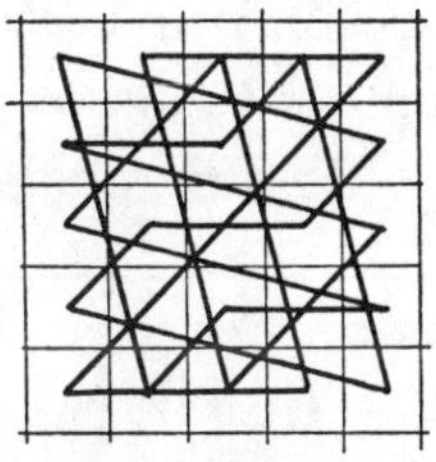

COMPLETED 5 X 5 SQUARE AND ITS MAGIC LINE

FORMATION OF THE 5 X 5 SQUARE BY MEANS OF DIAGONAL SQUARE THE VACANT CELLS OF WHICH ARE FILLED BY TRANSFERRING NUMBERS FROM OUTSIDE TO INSIDE IN THE MANNER SHOWN

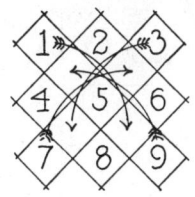

2	7	6
9	5	1
4	3	8

3 X 3 SQUARE AND ITS MAGIC LINE FORMED BY THE SAME METHOD

DIFFERENT MAGIC LINES IN THE SAME SQUARE

15	10	3	6
4	5	16	9
14	11	2	7
1	8	13	12

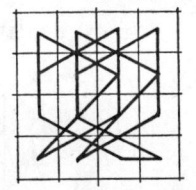

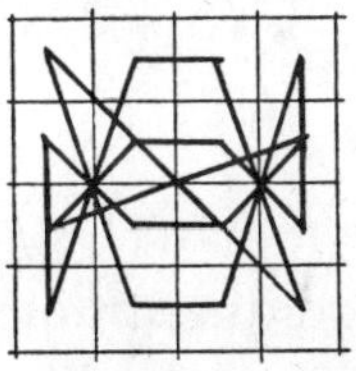

16	3	2	13
5	10	11	8
9	6	7	12
4	15	14	1

"GWALIOR" AND "MELANCHOLIA" 4 X 4 SQUARES AND THEIR MAGIC LINES FOUND BY FOLLOWING NUMBERS IN SEQUENCE

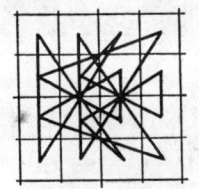

THE TWO MAGIC LINES FOUND BY FOLLOWING THE ALTERNATE NUMBERS — AN ODD SERIES AND AN EVEN: 1,3,5,7, ETC; AND 2,4,6,8 ETC

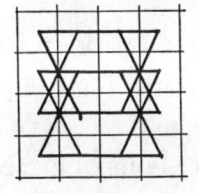

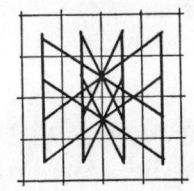

THE FOUR MAGIC LINES FOUND BY FOLLOWING THE NUMBERS WITH AN INTERVAL OF FOUR: 1,5,9,13,1, ETC, TWO ODD AND TWO EVEN.

ing of the first nine digits, three in each row, with a magic sum of 15. It is constructed according to the following method, applicable to all odd-number squares:

The numbers are first written in their natural order, in three rows of three each, so that the whole forms a square. Parallel diagonal lines are then drawn between the numbers with the effect of forming rectangular cells, every alternate cell being a blank. In the diagonal square of the same number of cells as there are numbers, of which five cells are already filled and the remaining four empty, these latter are filled, and the magic square formed, by transferring the four numbers remaining on the *outside* of this square to the corresponding position *inside and opposite* — as though rotated in the third dimension. The process is clearly shown in Illustration 41, and the resultant magic line obtained by following the numbers in their natural order.

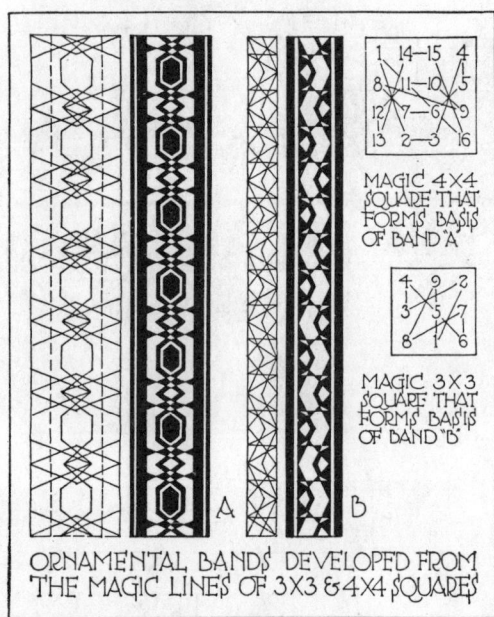

The ornamental band in Illustration 42 is directly derived from this line. Four of them, arranged about a common center, yield the pavement pattern shown in the headpiece to the next succeeding chapter. I made this magic line of 3 x 3, translated into a free-hand curve as shown in Illustration 8 and given the form of a Celtic interlace, do service as a ventilating grille in the ceiling of the Rochester Chamber of Commerce (Illustration 43), and I was much amused by the comment of a visiting eclectic architect: " Where did you get that design? I don't remember it in *Meyer's Handbook of Orna-*

ORNAMENT FROM MAGIC LINES IN MAGIC SQUARES

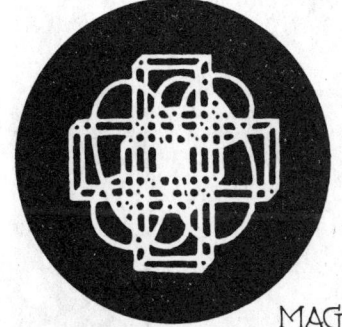

MAGIC LINE OF 3X3 SQUARE COMBINED WITH CUBES

PROJECTIVE ORNAMENT

ORNAMENT FROM MAGIC LINE OF 3X3

BOOK COVER DESIGN FROM MAGIC LINE IN 8X8 KNIGHT'S TOUR MAGIC SQUARE

BELOW: TEXTILE PATTERN FROM 5X5 SQUARE

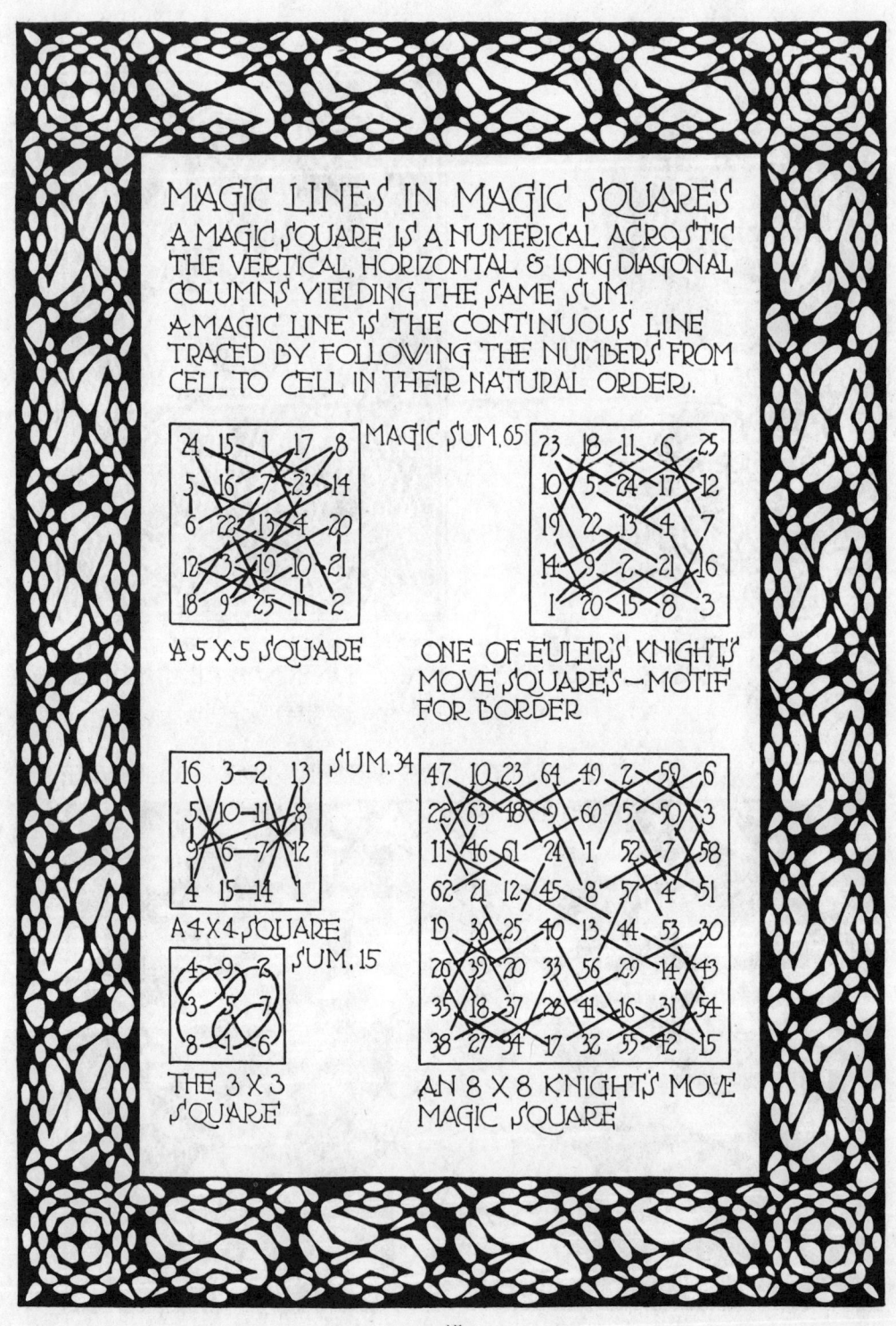

MAGIC LINES IN MAGIC SQUARES

A MAGIC SQUARE IS A NUMERICAL ACROSTIC THE VERTICAL, HORIZONTAL & LONG DIAGONAL COLUMNS YIELDING THE SAME SUM.
A MAGIC LINE IS THE CONTINUOUS LINE TRACED BY FOLLOWING THE NUMBERS FROM CELL TO CELL IN THEIR NATURAL ORDER.

MAGIC SUM, 65

A 5 X 5 SQUARE

ONE OF EULER'S KNIGHT'S MOVE SQUARES — MOTIF FOR BORDER

SUM, 34

A 4 X 4 SQUARE

SUM, 15

THE 3 X 3 SQUARE

AN 8 X 8 KNIGHT'S MOVE MAGIC SQUARE

45

ORNAMENT

ment. He appeared to feel that I had cheated because I had *not* used a crib. Two other decorative uses of this line are shown in Illustration 44.

There is another method of magic-square formation productive of what are known as knight's-move squares, so called because their magic path conforms to the knight's move on a chess-board — two squares forward and one to right or left. Examples of these knight's-move squares are shown in Illustration 45, one of 5 x 5, the magic line of which supplies the motif for the enclosing border, and the other of 8 x 8, whose line is developed into the book cover design shown in Illustration 44. The 5 x 5 magic line as a Celtic interlace is shown in Illustration 46. Other knight's-move squares account for the border of the title page of this volume, the elevator door in Illustration 47, and the cabinet doors in Illustration 48.

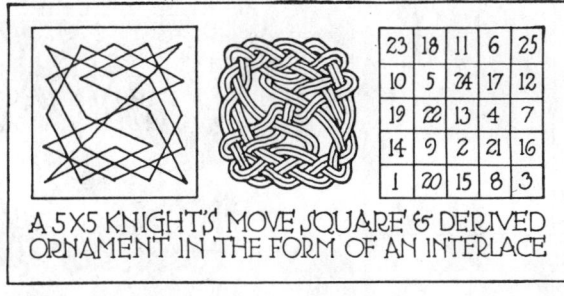

A 5X5 KNIGHT'S MOVE SQUARE & DERIVED ORNAMENT IN THE FORM OF AN INTERLACE

46

There is an altogether different way of using magic lines for the development of ornament — one which gives the æsthetic intuition freer play. This consists in repeating and reversing any given magic line, and these, in chess-board formation, yield a network which may be used as a warp for a great variety of patterns. The creative faculty has free play, yet by these means is subject to a control and direction which, because it is mathematical, makes for a beauty which is necessitous rather than fortuitous. Illustration 49 shows a number of 5 x 5 squares whose magic lines may be used in this way, and Illustrations 50 and 51 show textile patterns developed therefrom. Different designs may be thus derived from the same mathematical web. With the number of lines at one's disposal the possibilities of this variety of pattern-making are inexhaustible.

The number of different magic lines at the disposal of the designer is indeed without limit. To the mind uninitiated to the wonder-world of mathematics it might seem remarkable that there is even *one* arrangement of the first sixteen numbers in square form in which the vertical, horizontal, and diagonal columns will yield the same sum, 34, but it has

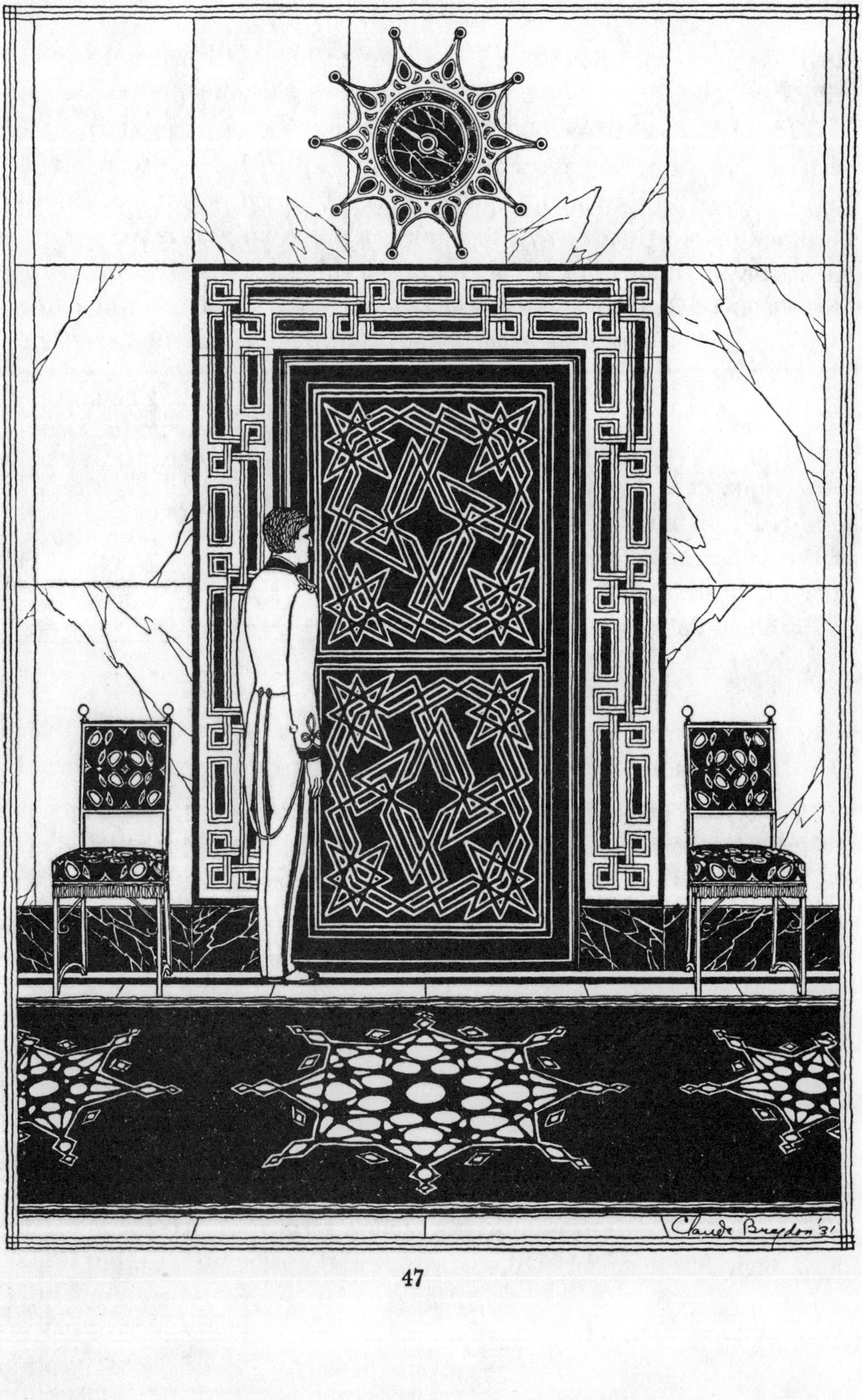
Claude Bragdon '31

48

been estimated that there are no less than 384 such arrangements, each one having, of course, a different magic line. Furthermore, from every one of such squares *more than one magic line can be developed.* For in addition to the line resulting from following the numbers in their natural order — 1, 2, 3, etc. — two other lines result from following from cell to cell the odd numbers and the even — 1, 3, 5, etc., and 2, 4, 6, etc. Nor is this all: four more lines reveal themselves by using an interval of four — 1, 5, 9, 13; 2, 6, 10, 14, etc. Such lines, being reciprocally related, sometimes make more interesting patterns than the magic line of the ordinary sort. Take, for example, the "Melancholia" 4 x 4 square (so called because represented in Dürer's etching by that name) represented in Illustration 41. Its magic line is not without interest, but the *two* lines made by following alternate numbers make a far more pleasing pattern; while the *four* lines made by using an interval of four yield truly symmetrical figures and are the most promising decorative material of all. Exactly the same thing is true of the "Gwalior" square (so called because inscribed on the lintel of the gate of the fort at Gwalior, India), also shown in Illustration 41. The leaded glass design in Illustration 52 and the rug pattern in Illustration 48 are derived from lines from these two squares.

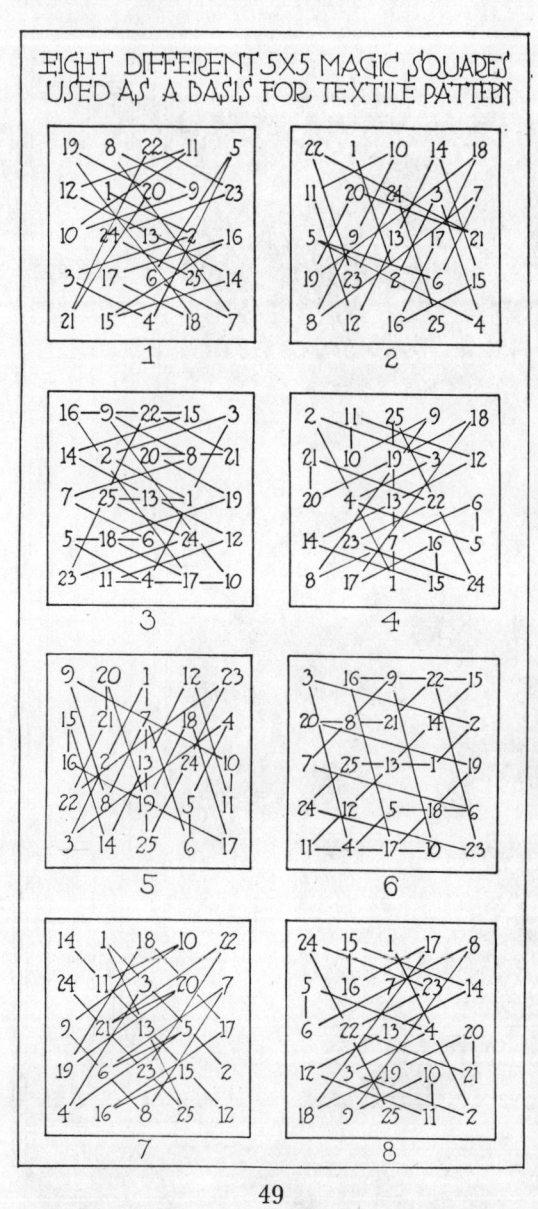

In general, magical arrangements of numbers result from transpositions and rotations whereby a kind of balance or polarization is established, making a magic square as different from any other similar arrangement of numbers as a horseshoe magnet is different from a horse's shoe. This polarity is indicated by the magic line in a manner analogous to the way magnetism in a magnet is revealed by the shape assumed by iron filings laid within its field of attraction. Magic lines are a legitimate and useful aid to the designer of ornament, but care should be taken not to use them slavishly. One's personal and intuitive feeling for rhythm and beauty should be the final arbiter.

A WINDOW OPENING INTO THE WORLD OF THE WONDROUS

7 4

6 5

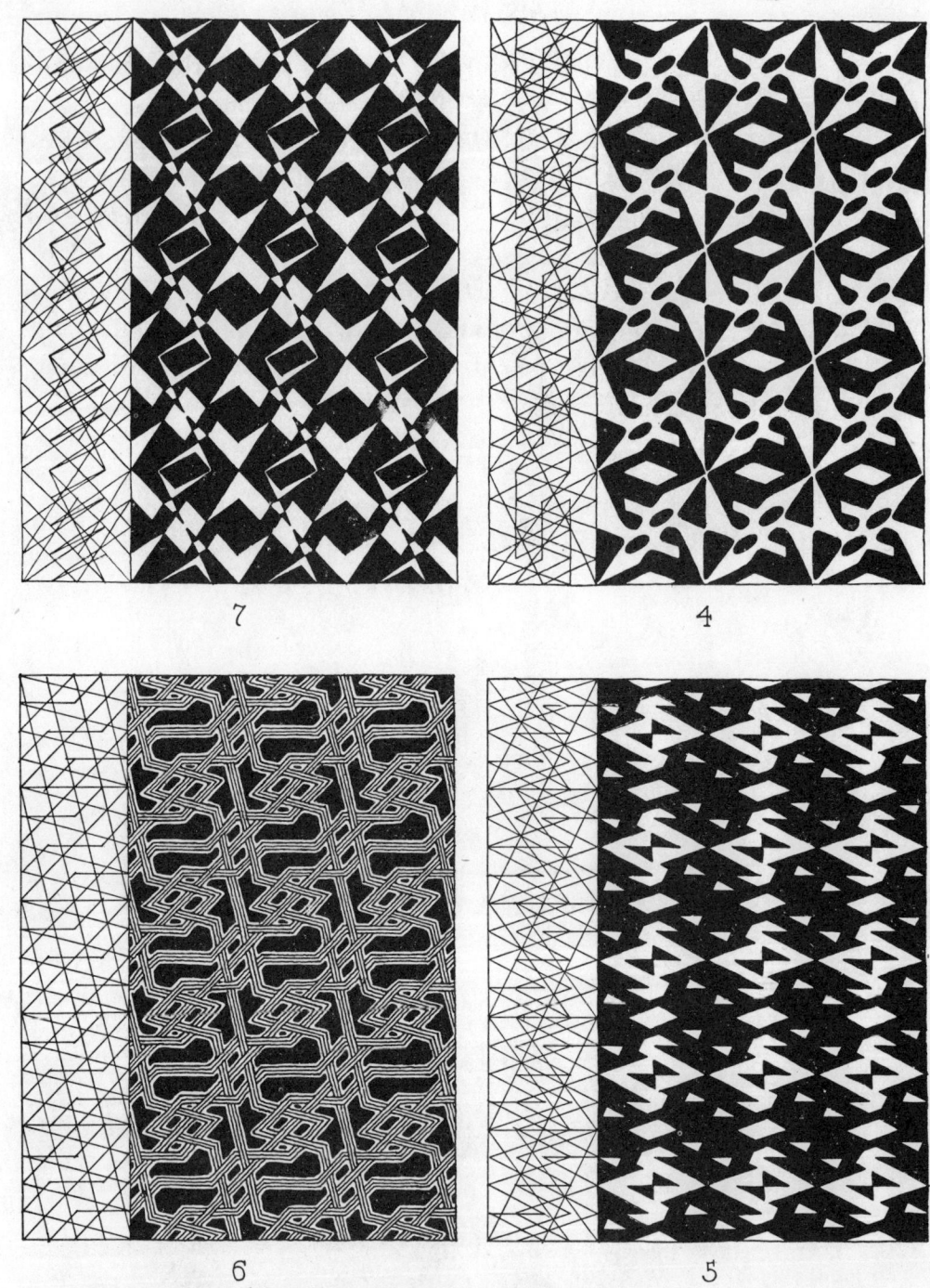

THE NUMBERS REFER TO SQUARES SHOWN IN THE TEXT ILLUSTRATION
TEXTILE PATTERNS DERIVED FROM MAGIC LINES IN 5X5 SQUARES

LEADED GLASS—MOTIF: THE DODECAHEDRON IN PLANE PROJECTION, UNITS LINKED TOGETHER

ENCAUSTIC TILE—MOTIF THE DODECAHEDRON

5

4

DESIGNS DERIVED FROM THE PLANE PROJECTION OF ONE OF THE PLATONIC SOLIDS AND FROM MAGIC LINES IN MAGIC 5×5 SQUARES

51

Claude Bragdon

ORNAMENT

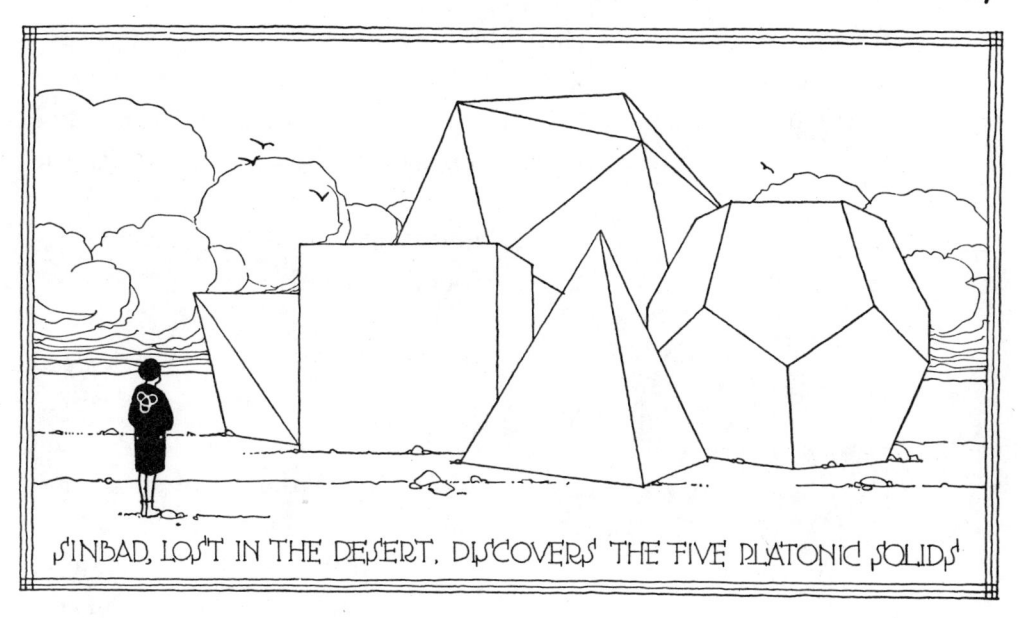

SINBAD, LOST IN THE DESERT, DISCOVERS THE FIVE PLATONIC SOLIDS

THE PLATONIC SOLIDS

A second profitable source of ornament I found in the so-called Platonic solids. The unique, the archetypal character of these regular polyhedrons of three-dimensional space has been recognized from the most ancient times. Among the playthings of the infant Bacchus were " dice " in the form of the five Platonic solids, the implication being that upon these patterns all things in the universe are built. Plato assigns four of them to the four elements, earth, fire, air, and water, and the vessel which contains them all he conceived to be the sphere, which he identified with the dodecahedron because of its approximation to the spherical form. The Platonic solids are the only regular polyhedrons which, assembled together each after its own kind, would fill three-dimensional space — or any portion of it — without a remainder.

Here, then, is mathematical truth; here is significant form; how may the Platonic solids be made to yield the thing we seek? Nature herself gives the needed hint, having seemingly pre-empted these very shapes for her own pattern-making, along with the ovoid and the logarithmic spiral, as the study of flowers and crystals makes plain. We have only to follow nature's method — not slavishly following her patterns, but creating, with the same data, new patterns of our own.

The first thing to do is to become thoroughly familiar with these five forms. By name they are the tetrahedron, the hexahedron (or cube), the octahedron, the dodecahedron, and the icosahedron, having respectively four, six, eight, twelve, and twenty polygonal faces, as shown in Illustration 54. A good way to get to know these forms is to make paper models of them according to the familiar kindergarten method of cutting, folding, and pasting. The lower portion of the illustration shows them developed on a plane — in their unfolded form. Better than cardboard or clay models would be replicas of them made of glass, for then by looking *through* them, seeing the far side simultaneously with the near, the interrelationships of the lines formed by the joining of their bounding surfaces could be studied from the point of view of *pattern*. The same thing can be done almost equally well, however, by means of plane projections. A number of such projections are shown at the right of Illustration 54. For convenience of identification the far sides of the figures are shown in dotted lines and the near side in solid.

MOTIF, THE PROJECTED DODECAHEDRON
53

The translation of these unfolded and projected Platonic solids into ornament is possible because they too, like magic lines, are graphic representations of significant mathematical truths. Of such truths beauty is,

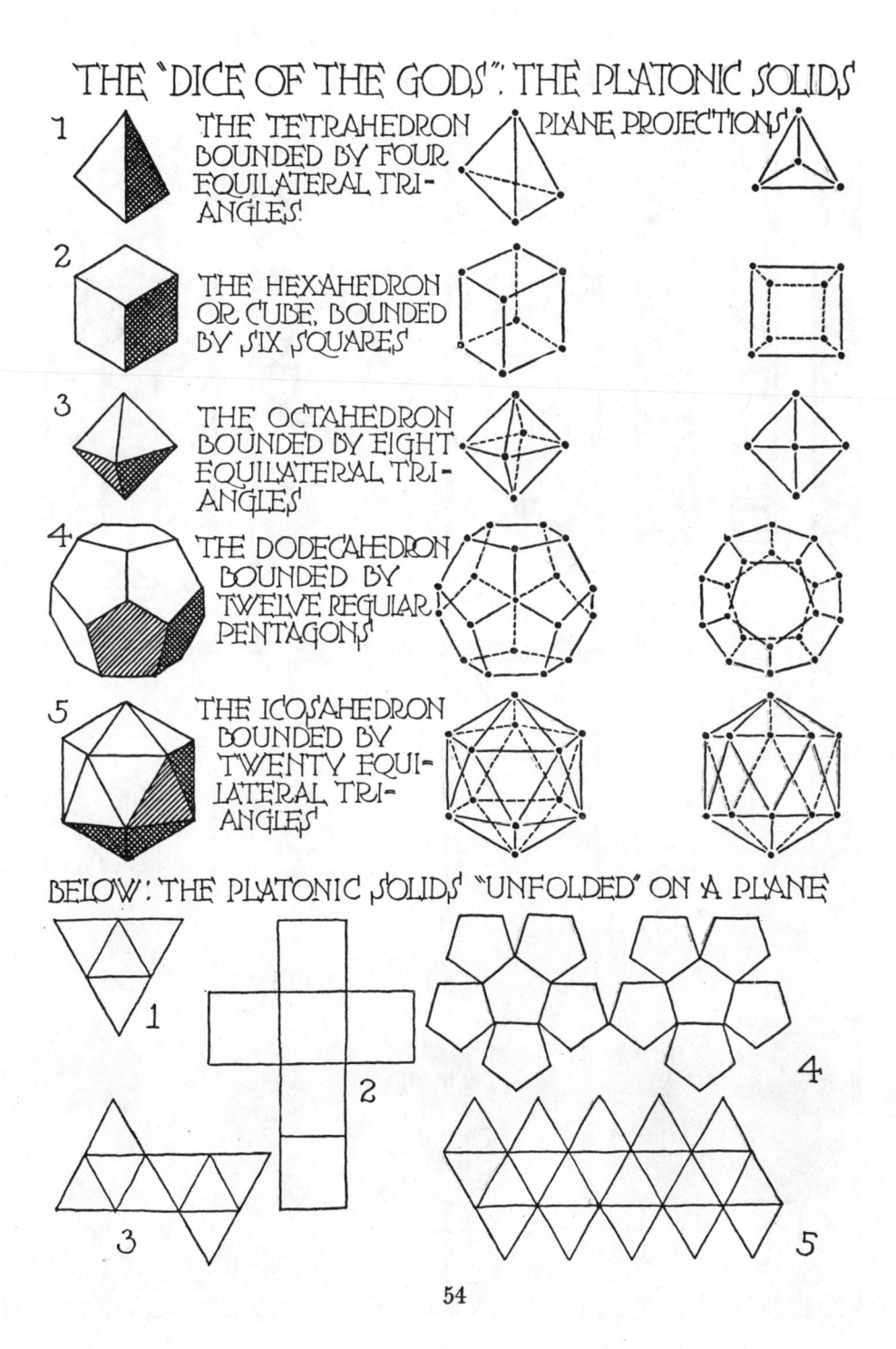

THE "DICE OF THE GODS": THE PLATONIC SOLIDS

PLANE PROJECTIONS

1. THE TETRAHEDRON BOUNDED BY FOUR EQUILATERAL TRIANGLES

2. THE HEXAHEDRON OR CUBE, BOUNDED BY SIX SQUARES

3. THE OCTAHEDRON BOUNDED BY EIGHT EQUILATERAL TRIANGLES

4. THE DODECAHEDRON BOUNDED BY TWELVE REGULAR PENTAGONS

5. THE ICOSAHEDRON BOUNDED BY TWENTY EQUILATERAL TRIANGLES

BELOW: THE PLATONIC SOLIDS "UNFOLDED" ON A PLANE

THE PLATONIC SOLIDS AS MOTIFS FOR ORNAMENT

1   2   3   4   5

5   1

1 AND 4 "UNFOLDED" AS A FRAME FOR FLORAL FORMS

55

56

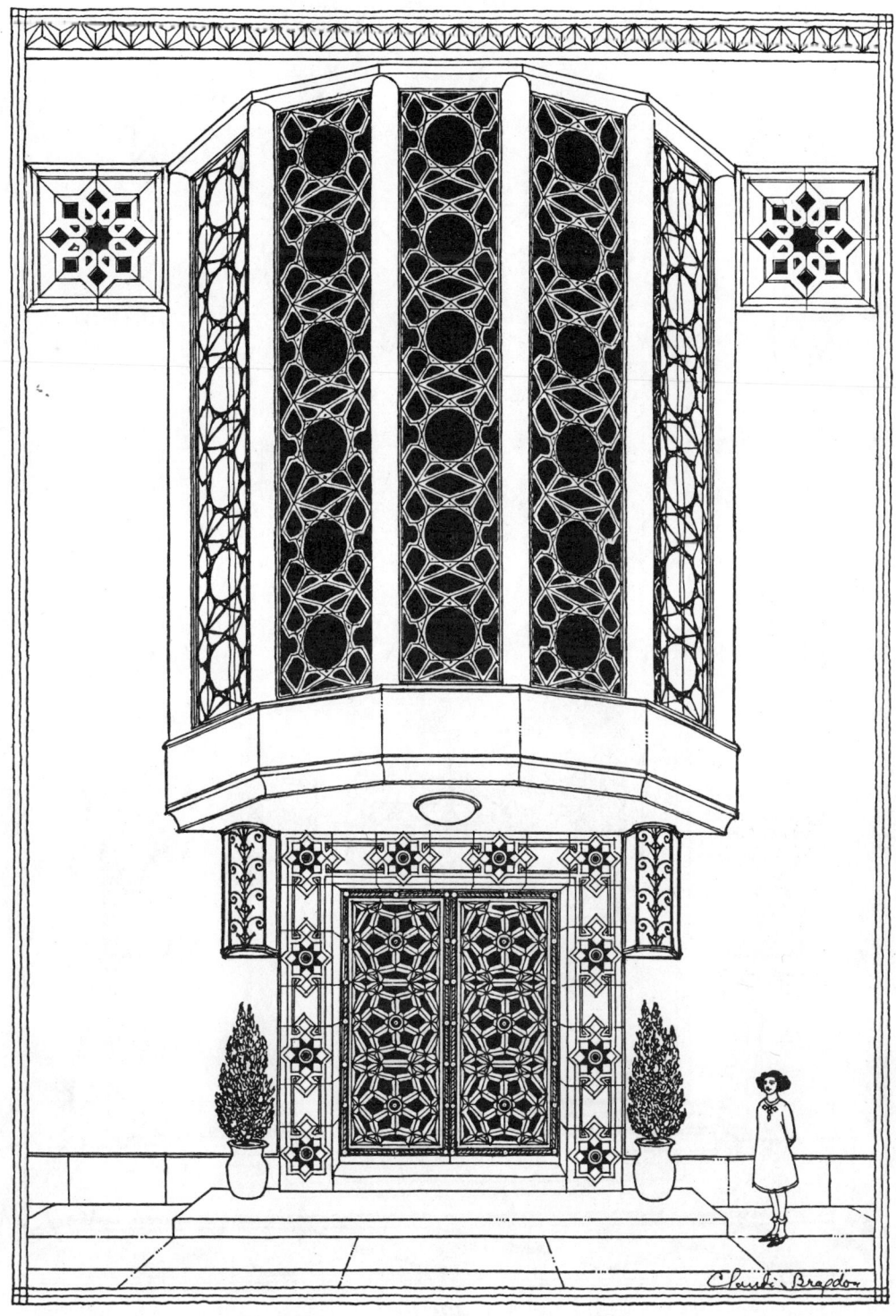

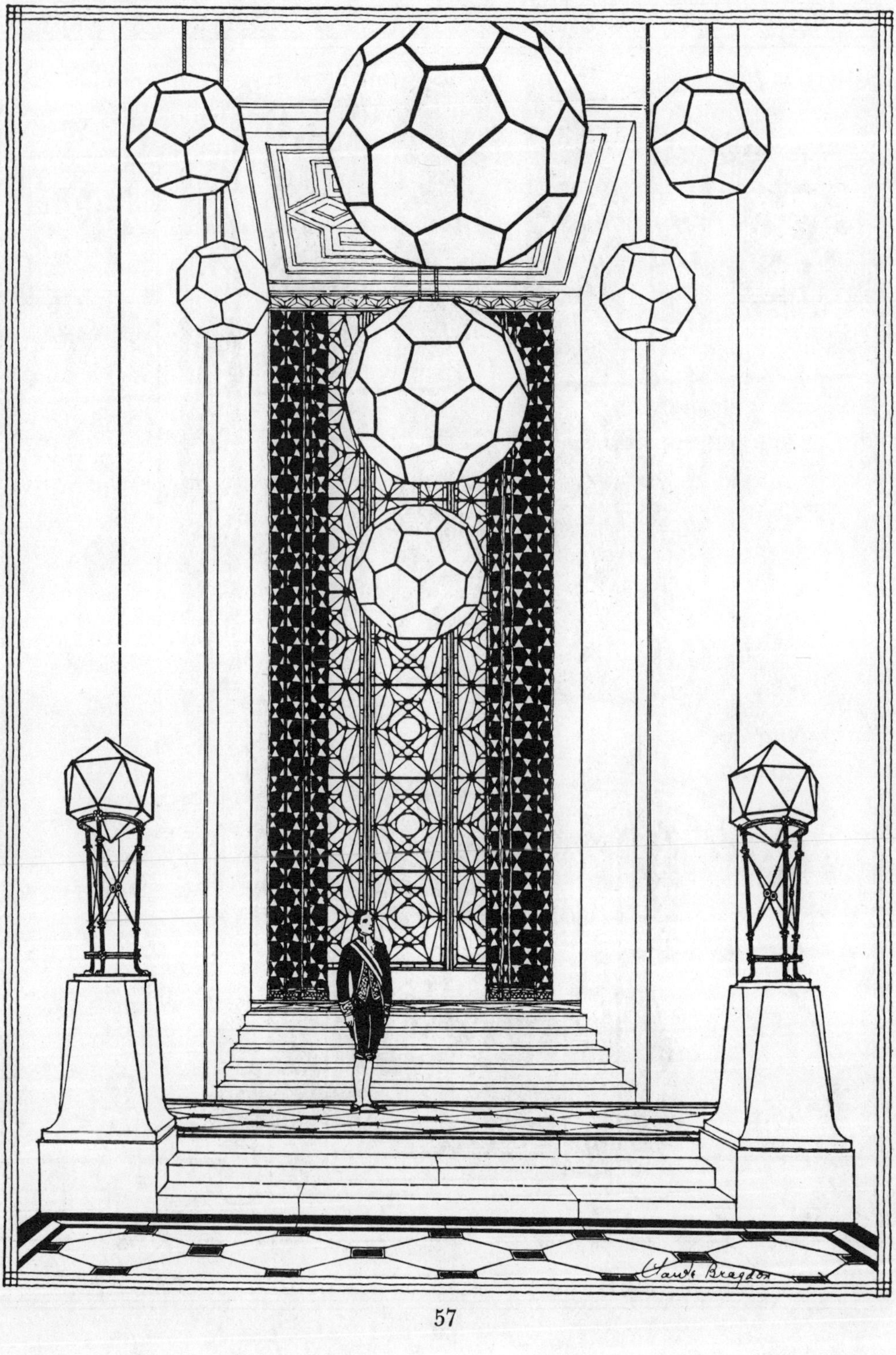
Claude Bragdon

ORNAMENT

as it were, the *shadow*, a thing invisible until its shape and presence be revealed by something upon which it can be cast. The shadow of a magic square is its magic line, and the shadow of a Platonic solid is the network of lines made by its plane projection. Illustration 55 shows the direct translation of these into ornament, and Illustration 56 the same thing achieved with more subtlety and success. The design for the doors is derived from one plane projection of the dodecahedron, and that of the glass-work in the bay window above from another. Illustration 53 shows the same door design but to a larger scale. Illustration 57 shows a leaded glass pattern derived from a projection of the icosahedron not shown on the page of diagrams, but easily identifiable. The lighting fixtures which are so prominent a feature of this drawing are in the form of icosahedrons and dodecahedrons, the largest being a semi-regular polyhedron bounded by pentagons and hexagons. The ornamental motif used throughout Illustration 58 is the icosahedron, in its three-dimensional form in the terminals to the parapet, and two-dimensionally in the gates.

Doubtless much more and much better ornament than any here shown can be derived, directly or indirectly, from the Platonic solids, but these examples sufficiently demonstrate that such significant and symmetrical forms can be used as ornamental motifs, and that by the skilful use of such material the designer is able to create beauty beyond his personal power of evocation. It cannot be too often insisted, however, that success depends less on a slavish adherence to the particular linear *web* selected than upon the æsthetic sensitivity which prompts departures from it and the free use of it only as a substructure. Mathematical aids to design, like the machine in industry, should ever be subservient to the human spirit, not an enslaver of it. Greek athletes are said to have rubbed their bodies with sand and oil: In this connection mathematics may be thought of as the sand and æsthetic intuition as the oil.

ENTRANCE TO A MAUSOLEUM—ORNAMENT DERIVED FROM THE PLATONIC SOLIDS, THE TETRAHEDRON AND ICOSAHEDRON

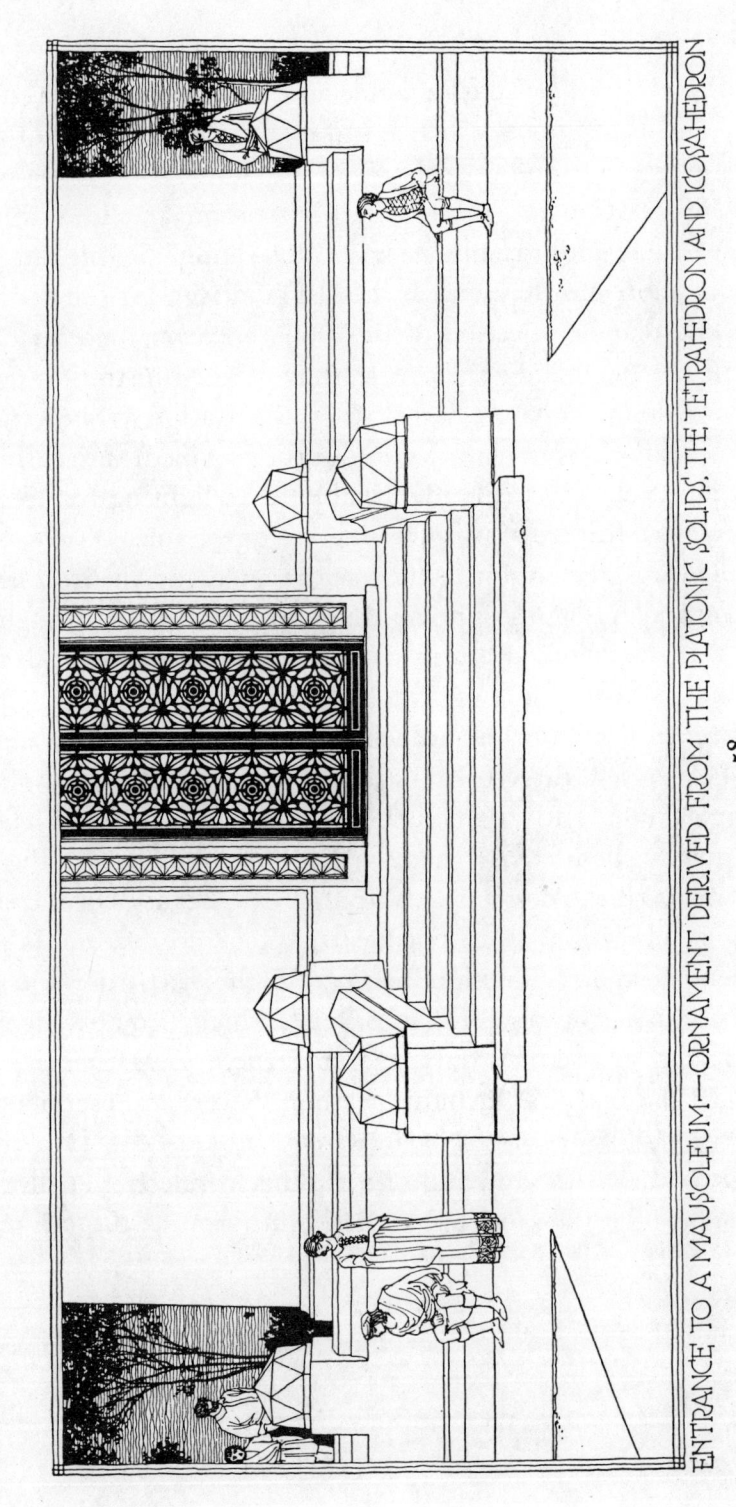

ORNAMENT

HYPERSOLIDS IN PLANE PROJECTION

The third source of ornament is an extension of the second (the plane projections of the Platonic solids), but an extension in a new direction — a direction at right angles to every known direction — into the fourth dimension, in point of fact.

Now although the fourth dimension may be only a fairy-tale of mathematics, it can be made use of by the designer of ornament, and this particular use constitutes, it seems to me, a contribution to his armory of no small interest and importance. Such also is the opinion of architect C. Howard Walker — himself the author of a book on ornament. In a review of *Projective Ornament* he says:

Mr. Bragdon's knowledge of geometry has led him to an initial application which is practically a discovery of a hitherto unused method of enriching geometrical design. It is a very valuable addition to the *formulæ* of a designer. Among the chief faults in geometric design have been the paucity of detail and meagre modulations of varying scale. In order to obtain this, subdivisions of an unimaginative type or else mere filling patterns in geometric units have been adopted. The development in the fourth dimension has filled these needs without resorting to either subterfuge. It is a development which greatly enriches the geometric *foci* and creates its own detail. Modulation and variation of scale occur naturally in every case, and monotony is diminished.

Now the world of the fourth dimension is a paradoxical world, and its forms are in a literal sense fantastic, but they are *mathematically true* nevertheless, and this is the only kind of truth which need concern us in this connection. The regular hypersolids of four-dimensional space — analogous to the Platonic solids of three-dimensional space — are the "fantastic forms" which will prove most useful to the designer of ornament. The number and relative positions of the vertices, edges, plane sides, and bounding solids of these hypersolids can be as accurately known *to the mind* as the Platonic solids themselves. And although it is impossible to *visualize* them, by a process analogous to the perspective method (by means of which a three-dimensional object is represented in plane projection) they can be reduced to linear diagrams. Such representations, enormously more rich and various than the plane projections of the Platonic solids themselves, constitute this third source of ornament.

For a description of the method whereby these two-dimensional representations of four-dimensional forms is achieved the reader is referred to the following chapter; here I shall give only a concise record of the use I have made of them, with representations of a few of the achieved results.

Illustration 59 shows the pentahedroid, the octahedroid, and the hexadecahedroid in plane projection. These are the four-dimensional correlatives of the tetrahedron, the hexahedron, and the octahedron. That they are full of decorative possibilities is evident at a glance: they *are* ornament. The rug design in Illustration 47 was determined by two of them, and the rug in Illustration 60 was based upon four octahedroids represented as cubes within cubes with vertices joined, as shown in Illustration 61, which gives also the source of the sofa-covering — a hexacosihedroid. The wall-hanging in Illustration 48 was derived from a different projection of this same hypersolid — of six hundred sides. It is represented entire in the intricate diagram at the bottom of Illustration 59. It alone constitutes an exhaustless mine of beauty into which I have repeatedly delved. Practically every pattern in the frontispiece of this volume was derived, directly or remotely, from this 600-hedroid in one or another of its presentments, and the sunburst surrounding the clock in Illustration 62 is made up of certain of its constituent parts. Indeed, it might almost be said of this figure that it is itself the womb of a new ornamental mode. Illustration 63 represents a pair of doors the panels of which are decorated with patterns derived from projected hypersolids.

The so-called artistic temperament has an aversion, sometimes amounting to a subjective fear, to everything which savors of the mathematical, seeming to sense in it something inimical to the free play of the creative imagination. But this is an attitude born either of ignorance or of educational malpractice. There is nothing so liberating to the spirit and stimulating to the imagination as the intention of consciousness upon geometry and number. Approached in the right way, mathematics becomes not the ravisher but the lover, the bringer of light and of delight, the fecundator of new forms of beauty. And if the reader says, " All this is above my head," I can only answer, " No, it is close beside your hand! "

REGULAR POLYHEDROIDS OF FOUR DIMENSIONAL SPACE
IN PLANE PROJECTION, CORRELATIVES OF THREE PLATONIC SOLIDS

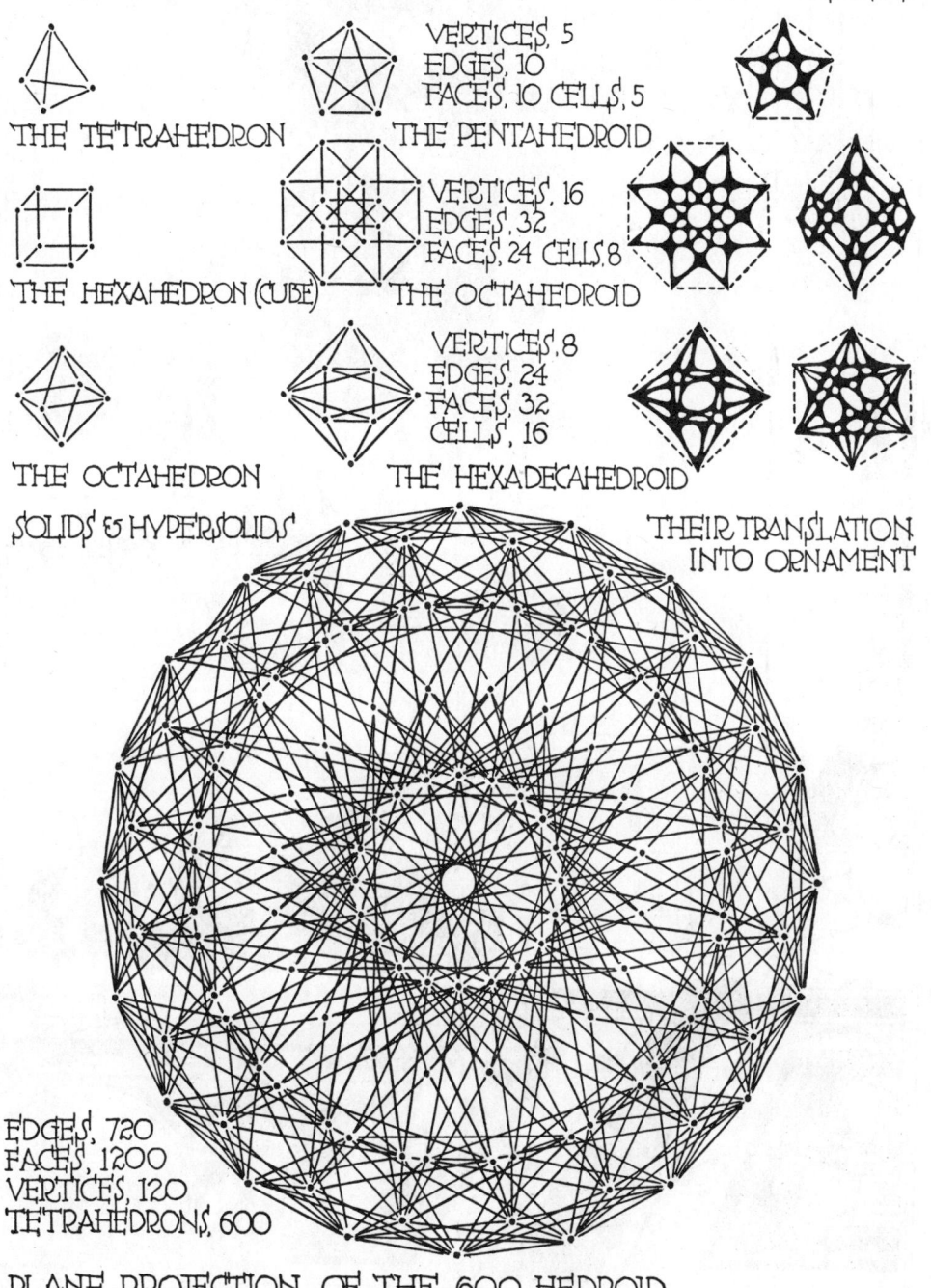

THE TETRAHEDRON

THE PENTAHEDROID
VERTICES, 5
EDGES, 10
FACES, 10 CELLS, 5

THE HEXAHEDRON (CUBE)

THE OCTAHEDROID
VERTICES, 16
EDGES, 32
FACES, 24 CELLS, 8

THE OCTAHEDRON

THE HEXADECAHEDROID
VERTICES, 8
EDGES, 24
FACES, 32
CELLS, 16

SOLIDS & HYPERSOLIDS

THEIR TRANSLATION INTO ORNAMENT

EDGES, 720
FACES, 1200
VERTICES, 120
TETRAHEDRONS, 600

PLANE PROJECTION OF THE 600 HEDROID

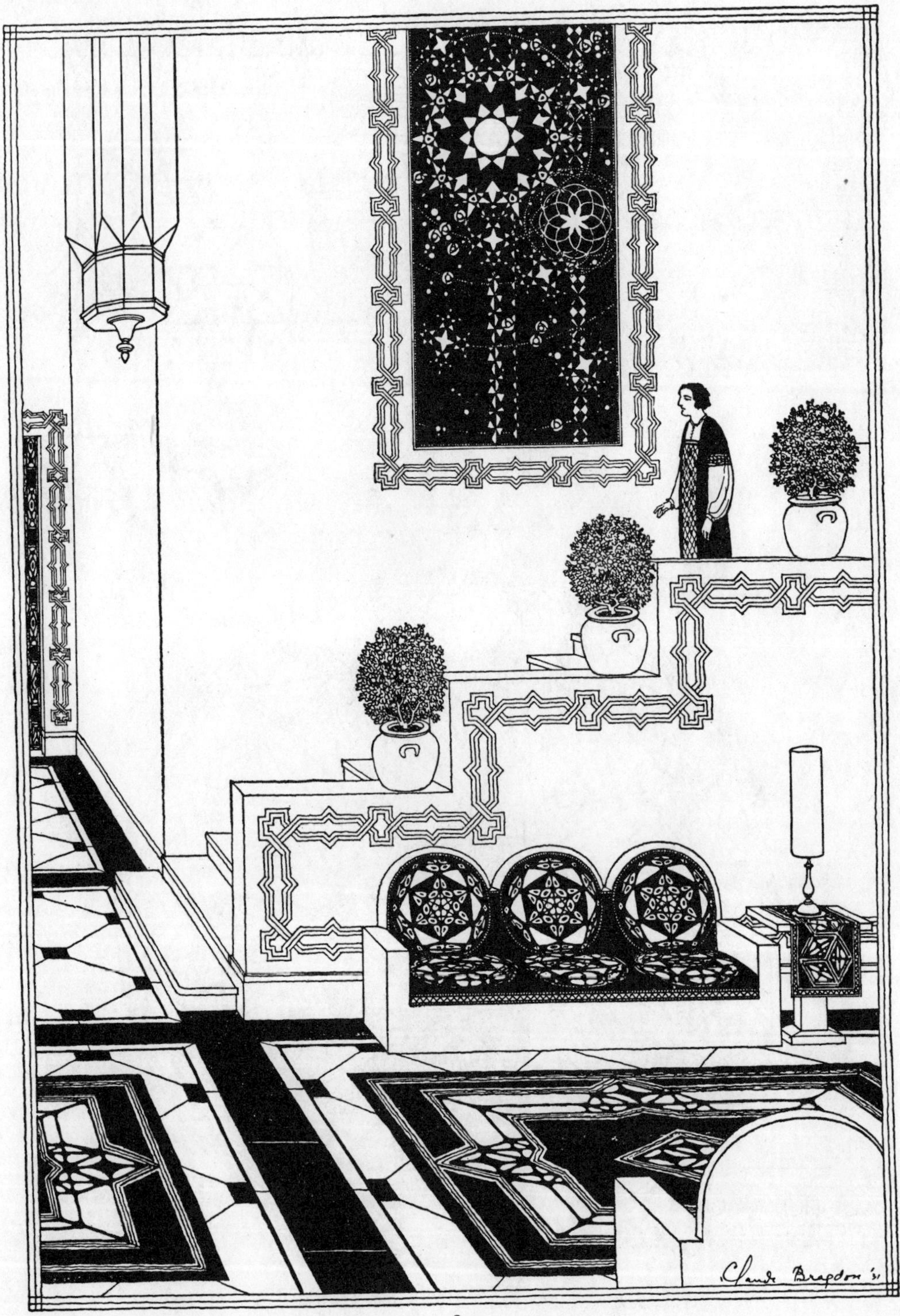
Claude Bragdon '31

VARIOUS ORNAMENTAL PATTERNS: THEIR DERIVATION.

THE HEXACOSIHEDROID

HYPER CUBES

MAGIC LINES OF 3X3, 4X4

HEXADECAHEDROID

HEXACOSIHEDROID

62

ENTRANCE·DOORWAY
FOR·ORCHESTRA·SETTING

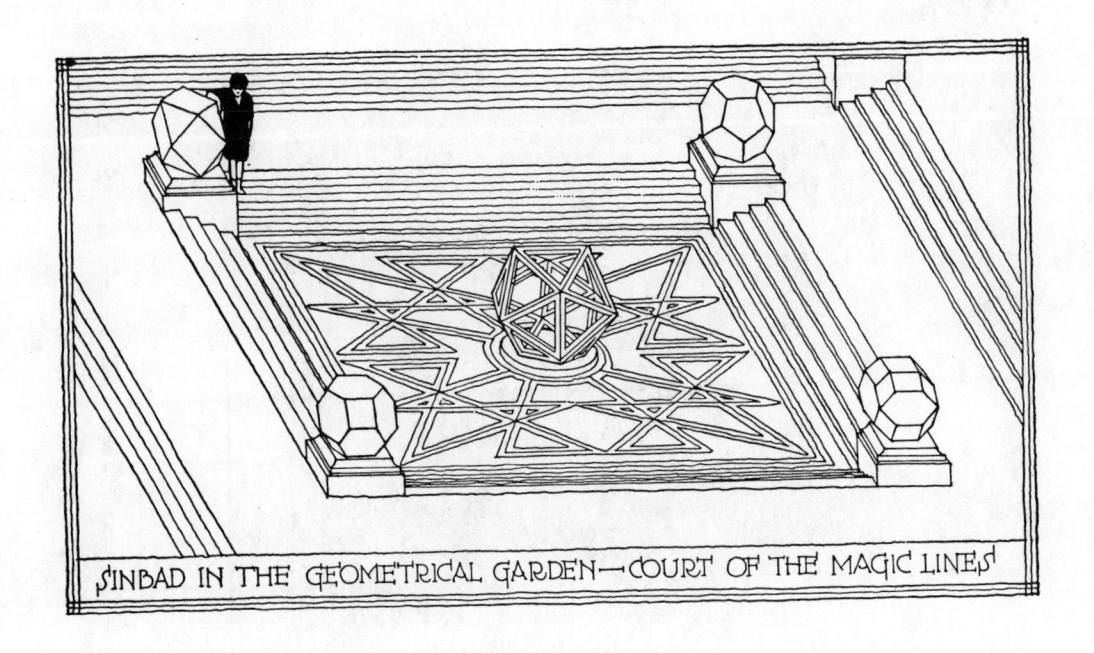

SINBAD IN THE GEOMETRICAL GARDEN—COURT OF THE MAGIC LINES

VIII
TO BE SKIPPED BY THE CASUAL READER

ANYTHING in the nature of a treatise on magic-square formation or the projection of hypersolids would be out of place in a book of this sort, solely devoted to the discussion of certain æsthetic problems which beset the architectural designer. Nevertheless, to avoid the reproach of dealing with cryptograms to which the key is withheld, and to allay, if not altogether to satisfy, a natural curiosity, these subjects will be briefly dealt with. Should the reader desire to pursue them further, he has only to refer to the available literature about them.

In addition to the method of magic-square formation contained in the preceding chapter two others will now be given. For this I can do no better than quote a part of my essay in *The New Image* entitled: " Man, the Magic Square ":

Magic squares may be constructed in many different ways: The following is the so-called knight's-move method applied to a square of 5 x 5.

TO BE SKIPPED BY THE CASUAL READER 103

No special significance need be attached to the knight's move, it being only one of many systems of regular spacing, all of which will produce equivalent results. To chess-players the knight's move will need no explaining, but to those not familiar with the game it may be described as a move of two squares straight forward in any direction and one square to right or left. In this case the move is assumed to be uniformly upward and to the right.

The method consists in constructing parts of auxiliary squares around one or more sides of the main square and temporarily writing the numbers in the cells of these auxiliary squares when their regular spacing carries them outside the limits of the main square. The temporary location of these numbers in the cells of the auxiliary squares will then indicate into which cells of the main square they must be permanently transferred.

Illustration 64 shows a 5 x 5 main square with parts of three auxiliary squares. Starting with 1 in the center of the top line, the first knight's move of two cells upward and one to the right takes 2 across the top margin of the main square into the second cell of one of the auxiliary squares, so 2 must be transferred to the same relative position in the main square. Starting again from 2 in the main square, the next move places 3 within the main square, but 4 goes out of it into the lower left-hand corner of an auxiliary square, from which it must be transferred to the same location in the main square. 5 again falls within the main square, but when we come to 6, it is seen to fall within a cell already occupied by a number. This involves a departure from normal spacing known as "break" moves. In the present instance the break will be one square downward: that is, the number 6 will be made to fall in the cell immediately below 5, and this process is to be repeated whenever the same condition recurs. By referring to the appropriate diagram in illustration 64 it will be seen just where, and between what numbers, the break will be.

SHOWING WHERE "BREAKS" OCCUR

FORMATION OF A 5 X 5 MAGIC SQUARE BY THE "AUXILIARY SQUARE" METHOD

ORDINARY ORDER   REVERSE-ORDINARY   COMPLETED SQUARE

FORMATION OF A 4 X 4 MAGIC SQUARE BY THE "ORDERS OF WRITING" METHOD

64

Having filled all the cells according to this rule, observe the result: The sum of each of the five horizontal, five perpendicular, and two corner diagonal columns is 65, the magic sum. Also, the sum of any two numbers that are geometrically equidistant from the center is 26, or twice the number of the center cell, thus conforming to all the general conditions of a perfect square. But these do not exhaust its magic properties. If the reader will imagine the top and bottom edges of the square bent backward horizontally until they meet, thus forming a cylinder, he will discover that each spiral row of figures, traced either right-handed or left-handed, amounts to 65. And if the square be then bent vertically instead of horizontally, forming a cylinder of which the two sides, instead of the two ends, are joined, these spiral rows, either right-handed or left-handed, also add to 65. In the vertical cylinder there are five right-handed and five left-handed spirals, two of which form the corner diagonal columns across the square, leaving eight new combinations. The same number of combinations will also be found in the horizontal cylinder. Counting, therefore, five horizontal columns, five vertical columns, two corner diagonal columns, and sixteen right- and left-handed spiral columns, there will be found in all twenty-eight columns, each of which will sum up to 65.

The rules which govern even magic-square formation are altogether different from those which govern odd ones. The method chosen for observation involves two "orders" or methods of arrangement of figures, the *ordinary,* and the *reverse-ordinary* — *o* and *ro,* for short. The first is simply the ordinary way of writing the figures, arranged in square form, from right to left, and downward. The second proceeds from the lower right-hand corner to the left and upward, beginning where the ordinary arrangement ends and ending where that begins (Illustration 64). Or think of the *ro* square as derived from the *o* by a process of *mirroring* — a double rotation, the imaginary mirror being held on the right-hand edge of the *o* square, and this derived mirror-image again reversed by placing the glass on its upper edge, yielding the *ro* arrangement. In order to form the magic square shown in the illustration it is necessary to retain the numbers lying along the diagonals of the *o* square, for they add up to the magic sum, 34. In the remaining eight empty cells now substitute the numbers from the corresponding cells of the *ro* square. In the magic square thus formed every vertical and every horizontal row will add up to 34, thus fulfilling the minimum requirements of magic-square formation, but, as in the case of the 5 x 5 square, there are other similar summations: The four central numbers yield the magic sum, as do the four numbers which surround the center symmetrically. These five, added to the four vertical, four horizontal, and two diagonal summations, give a total of fifteen ways of obtaining the magic sum.

The formation of magic squares was a favorite preoccupation of the many-sided Benjamin Franklin, and the so-called Franklin squares are among the most ingenious ever developed. His 16 x 16 square, having a magic sum of 2,056, is shown in Illustration 65.

THE FAMOUS 16 X 16 "FRANKLIN" SQUARE

THE SUM OF THE 16 NUMBERS IN ANY ROW OR COLUMN IS 2056 —— THE SUM OF THE 8 NUMBERS IN HALF OF ANY ROW OR COLUMN IS 1028, OR ½ OF 2056 —— THE SUM OF THE NUMBERS IN TWO HALF-DIAGONALS IS 2056 —— THE SUM OF THE 4 CORNER NUMBERS AND THE 4 CENTRAL NUMBERS IS 1028 —— THE SUM OF THE NUMBERS IN ANY 16 CELLS WHICH ARE DISPOSED IN A SQUARE IS 2056

NOTE THE SEQUENCES IN ALTERNATE CELLS IN HORIZONTAL ROWS ALTERNATELY FROM LEFT TO RIGHT AND FROM RIGHT TO LEFT.

NOTE THE SUMMATIONS OF CELLS IN EACH ROW EQUIDISTANT FROM THE VERTICAL AXIS.

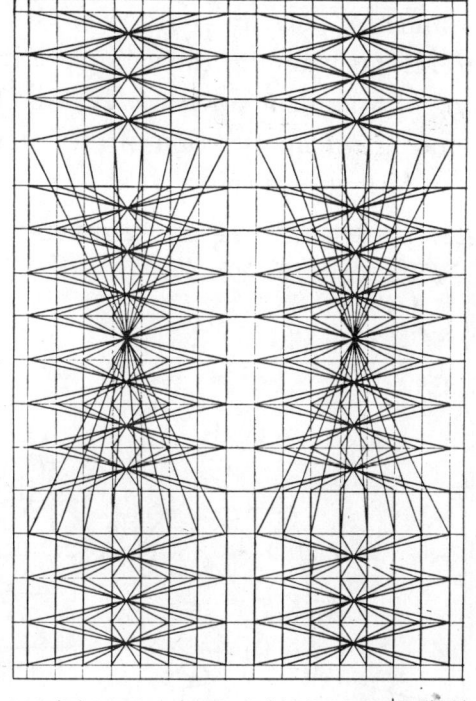

MAGIC LINE IN THE FRANKLIN 16-SQUARE BUT ELONGATED VERTICALLY ONE THIRD

65

Some of its amazing properties are noted underneath the drawing, but perhaps its most remarkable is the following: A square hole being cut in a piece of paper of such a size as to take in and show through it just sixteen of the little squares when laid on the greater square, the sum of the sixteen numbers so appearing through the hole, wherever placed on the greater square, will be 2,056, the magic sum. The method employed by Franklin in the construction of this square is not known, but W. S. Andrews, in his book, *Magic Squares and Cubes,* gives a key to the construction of squares belonging to the same class. To me the most interesting thing about this Franklin square is its magic line, shown in Illustration 65, for it translates a thing marvelous to the mind into a thing beautiful to the eye. The square itself, without the mathematical key of the magic sum, is only a meaningless conglomeration of apparently unrelated numbers; but the magic line reveals at a glance that here is order, symmetry, polarity — art, even, in the sense of *artfulness.* I am willing to rest my claim for the validity of the magic line as an aid in the designing of ornament upon the evidence of this line alone, because it is so convincing a demonstration of the interrelation between mathematical truth and formal beauty.

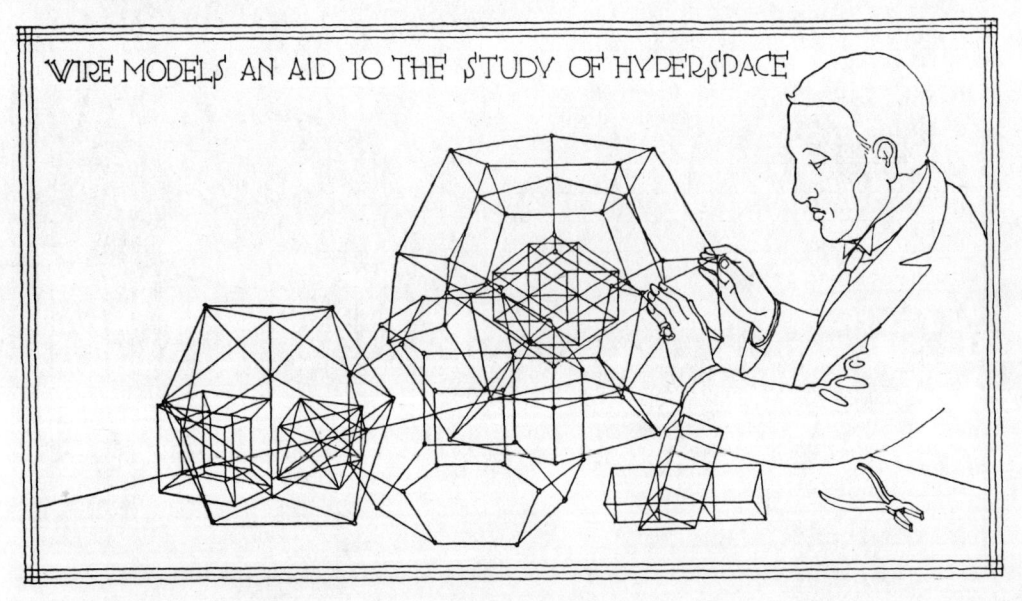

PLANE REPRESENTATIONS OF THREE PLATONIC HYPERSOLIDS

Let us approach the subject of the fourth dimension very simply, untroubled by any question of its reality or unreality: its *mathematical* reality is not open to question, and this is the only thing we need to know in order to go on. The geometry of four dimensions is as precisely formulated as is plane and solid geometry; like them, it is developed logically from axioms, and its problems are susceptible of the same sort of definition and proof. Four-dimensional geometry bears the same relation to solid geometry that the latter bears to plane geometry: a hypersolid is related to a solid in the same way that a solid is related to a plane; a hypersolid is bounded by solids just as a solid is bounded by planes. "But a solid cannot *be* a boundary!" shrieks outraged common sense. The mathematical mind, despite the absence of ocular evidence, finds no logical reason why it cannot, and four-dimensional geometry is the result. In defiance of all our observation and experience the mathematician posits a fourth perpendicular — a direction at right angles to every known direction — making four mutually independent perpendiculars instead of three. "Ridiculous! Preposterous! *Show* me that direction!" vociferates common sense. The answer might be that it is *time,* without which fourth co-ordinate it is impossible, in a kinetic universe, to establish the position of a body in space, but the mathematician assumes it to be a direction homogeneous and interchangeable with the three known dimensions of space, and proceeds with the development of a geometry founded upon this assumption.

By means of this geometry, although we cannot picture to ourselves the forms of hyperspace in the same way that we can picture those of ordinary space, we can build up in the mind a more or less precise conception of them. Indeed, by means of models and diagrams indicating the relations of their different parts, by studying their three-dimensional *cross-sections* and by a correlation of these sections it may be said that they *are* seen by the "mind's eye." Moreover, such exercises are highly beneficial to the designer, since they greatly stimulate and develop his intuition and imagination.

Limiting our discussion to the three simplest regular polyhedroids of four-dimensional space, the heptahedroid, the octahedroid, and the hexadecahedroid, the correlatives of the tetrahedron, the hexahedron, and the octahedron of three-dimensional space, there is this much that we may know (mathematically) about them:

1. *Each consists of equal regular polyhedrons together with their interiors, the polyhedrons being joined by their faces so as to enclose a*

portion of hyperspace, the hyperplane angles formed at the faces by the half-hyperplanes of adjacent polyhedroids being all equal to one another.

2. *The pentahedroid (hyper-tetrahedron) has 5 vertices, 10 edges, 10 faces, and 5 cells.*

The octahedroid or tesseract (hyper-hexahedron or hyper-cube) has 16 vertices, 32 edges, 24 faces, and 8 cells.

The hexadecahedroid or 16-hedroid (hyper-octahedron) has 8 vertices, 24 edges, 32 faces, and 16 cells.

3. *The faces of the pentahedroid are equilateral triangles, and its cells tetrahedrons.*

The faces of the hexahedroid are squares, and its cells hexahedrons.

The faces of the octahedroid are equilateral triangles, and its cells tetrahedrons.

With these data as a guide it will be possible to make linear diagrams of these hypersolids in the same way that one can make perspective representations of their three-dimensional correlatives, the first three Platonic solids. Such diagrams will of course be removed from their originals by two dimensions instead of one; that is to say, they will be perspectives of perspectives. Were they constructed as wire models (and this is not difficult), they would then bear the same relation to their four-dimensional correlatives that the plane representation of a solid bears to a solid.

As a preliminary exercise, in order to understand the method, let us first make diagrams of the tetrahedron, the hexahedron, and the octahedron, not from the visual memory of their appearance, but from a knowledge of their elements, for that is what we shall have to do when it comes to the four-dimensional figures. In other words, let us place ourselves in imagination in the position of a hypothetical plane-man to whom the third dimension is non-existent except as a concept — to whom plane figures are the " solids " of his two-dimensional space.

Were he required to represent a tetrahedron, or hyper-equilateral triangle, he would have first to consult his meta-geometry of three dimensions to find out what it could tell him about regular polyhedrons, quite in analogy with what four-dimensional geometry tells us about regular polyhedroids. It might read something like this:

A regular polyhedron of three-dimensional space consists of regular polygons together with their interiors, joined by their faces so as to enclose a portion of hyper- (three-dimensional) space, the angles formed by the half-planes of adjacent polygons being all equal to one another.

The tetrahedron has four vertices, all equally distant from one another, and it is bounded by four equilateral triangles.

His initial difficulty would be our own when trying to imagine the higher solids; namely: the impossibility of conceiving a solid of his space — in this case an equilateral triangle — as a *boundary*, and the paradox of the "third perpendicular," an independent direction definitely at right angles to the two dimensions of his plane.

First he draws an equilateral triangle, the base of the tetrahedron he proposes to represent. Its apex, he knows, must lie in the unknown direction, for in his space four independent and mutually equidistant points cannot exist. He therefore represents this apex as *projected* into his plane — anywhere, either inside or outside the limits of the triangle, and then, connecting this point with the vertices of the triangle by means of lines representing edges, he will have achieved as complete a representation of the tetrahedron as is possible in his space: the vertices are not all mutually equidistant, the angles are not all equal, three of the four bounding triangles are not truly equilateral, but vertices, edges, and sides are nevertheless of the right number and in the right relation to one another. We, to whom the tetrahedron is a familiar figure, recognize his representation, account for its discrepancies as due to perspective distortion — the changes incident to representing a three-dimensional object in two dimensions — and correct them mentally. But whatever mental correction he could make would be referable to no remembered sensuous image: the whole thing would lie for him in the domain of paradox. In exactly the same way the facts of four-dimensional geometry are paradoxical because they correspond to nothing in our experience.

Now, pursuing a similar method, let us attempt a diagram of a pentahedroid, or hyper-tetrahedron, from our knowledge of its elements and interrelations.

Being a regular hypersolid we know that its vertices would touch the hypersurface of a hypersphere at equidistant points. A sphere is the three-dimensional correlative of a hypersphere; a circle is the two-dimensional correlative of a sphere. The pentahedroid has five vertices, all mutually equidistant from one another. These we dispose circle-wise and equidistant — the fact that each is also equally distant from every other we are obliged to ignore. We then connect each of these vertices with every other by means of lines representing edges, and its representation

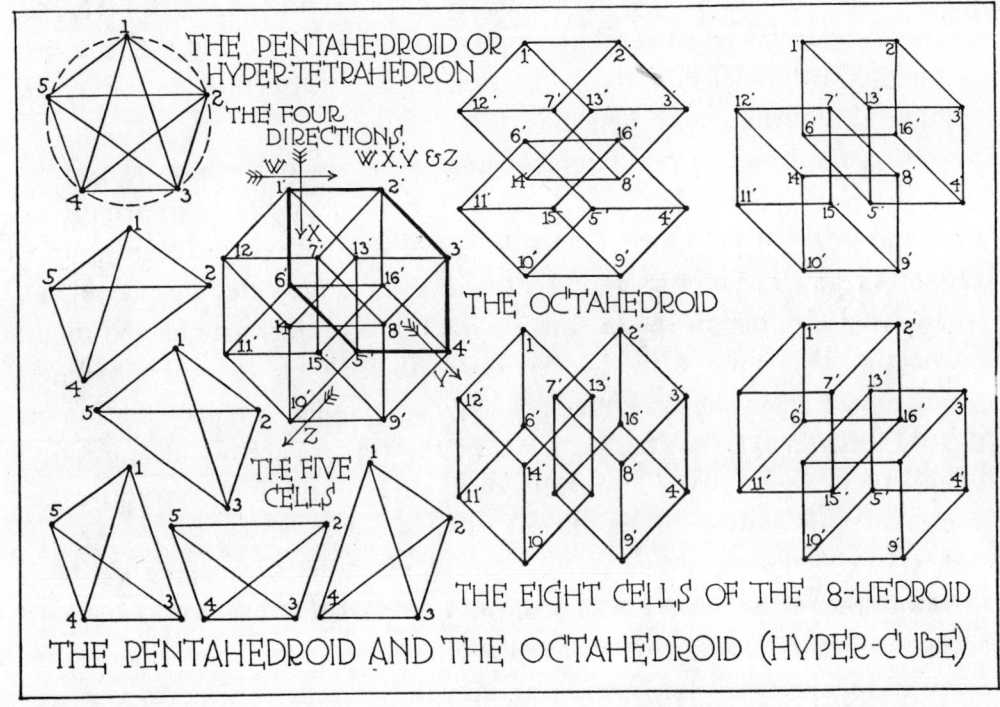

THE PENTAHEDROID AND THE OCTAHEDROID (HYPER-CUBE)

66

in a plane is thereby achieved; for it is possible to identify the ten edges, ten faces, and five cells. They have suffered inevitable distortions, due to the exigencies of representation; but save for this the diagram is mathematically correct (Illustration 66).

Let us next attempt the representation of an octahedroid or hypercube, using an extension of the method used to develop a cube from a square, which is by moving the square in a direction perpendicular to its plane through a distance equal to its edge. Similarly, the hypercube can be generated by the motion of a cube in a direction perpendicular to its hyperplane through a distance equal to its edge.

Start with the line: Moving it in a direction at right angles to itself a distance equal to its length develops a square. To move the square in a direction at right angles to its plane requires a third dimension not contained in the paper on which the drawing is made. It is necessary therefore to *represent* this third direction of movement *within* the plane of the paper: let us assume that it is diagonally downward to the right. This is not *really* at right angles to the plane, but it is the best we can do under the circumstances. Representing the square in its new position at the end of its movement into the third dimension, each vertex having traced out a line, we have achieved a familiar and recognizable representation of a cube on a plane. It has the required number of vertices (eight), of edges (eight), and six bounding squares, four of which have become lozenge-shaped through the exigencies of this kind of representation.

Now let us develop this cube into a hypercube. To do so it would have to move at right angles to all three of the dimensions of our space: that is, into the fourth dimension — into hypothetical space. Our space does not contain such a direction, but neither, be it remembered, does the plane-man's world contain the third dimension. We have overcome this difficulty once, let us overcome it again in the same way; let us establish this fourth direction as downward and to the left. This is actually at right angles to the direction in which the square was represented to have moved to generate the cube, which direction is in turn hypothetically at right angles to the first two. Thus we have represented the four mutually perpendicular axes of hyperspace. Drawing the cube in its new position (below and to the left) and connecting by lines its eight vertices with those of its prototype, we have achieved the representation of a hypercube. Barring distortions, it fulfils the requirements, for it has 16 vertices, 32 edges, 24 faces, and 8 cubical cells. These, occurring in pairs, can be identified without difficulty. For purposes of identification they are shown separately in Illustration 66.

There is another way of representing a tesseract by means of a diagram, corresponding to the one-vanishing-point perspective method. If a smaller square be drawn within the limits of a larger and the corresponding corners connected by lines, we have a one-point perspective of a cube, the smaller square representing its far side. Now draw a smaller cube within the limits of a larger, on the assumption that the fourth direction is *inward*, instead of, as in the former case, downward and to the left. Connect by lines the corresponding vertices of these two cubes and again we have a representation of a hypercube. The large cube represents the cube at the beginning of its movement into the fourth dimension; the smaller cube, at the end of that movement; and the six pie-tin-shaped solids having two faces in common with these cubes represent the six other cubes engendered by this movement into the fourth dimension. This diagram, like the other, fulfils the given requirements as to the number of vertices, edges, faces, and cells (Illustration 67).

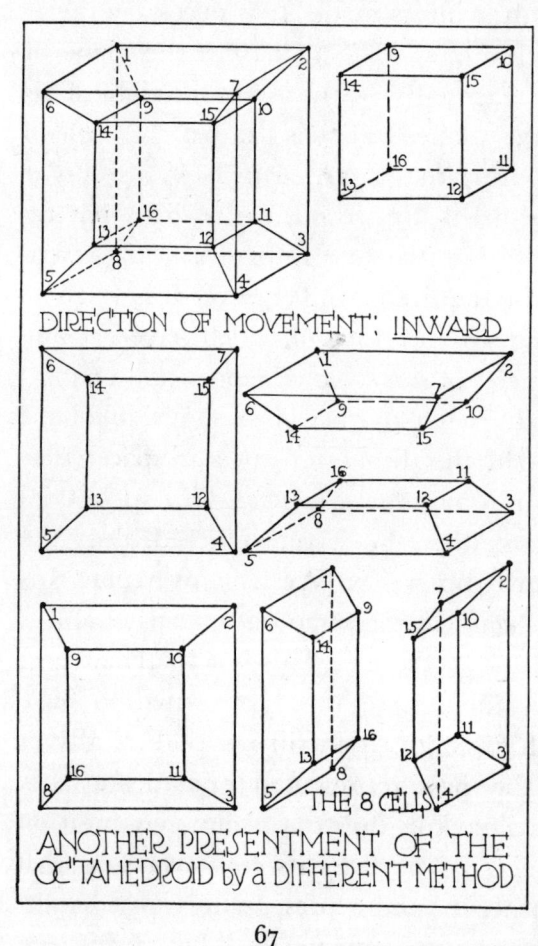

For our diagram of a hexadecahedroid let us begin with its three-dimensional correlative, the regular octahedron. And in order to get a more perfect understanding of this latter, consider it first in relation to the tetrahedron and the cube:

If diagonals be drawn on the faces of a cube, the six lines will form the edges of an inscribed regular tetrahedron, because the lines are necessarily of equal length and the angles also equal. The center of each one of these edges (diagonals) will in turn mark one apex of an inscribed regular octahedron; that is to say, the six points of the octahedron will touch the centers of the six faces of the cube (Illustration 68). The octahedron has twelve edges and eight triangular faces.

Connect the opposite apexes of the octahedron by means of lines passing through its center. These three axes are conceived of as being mu-

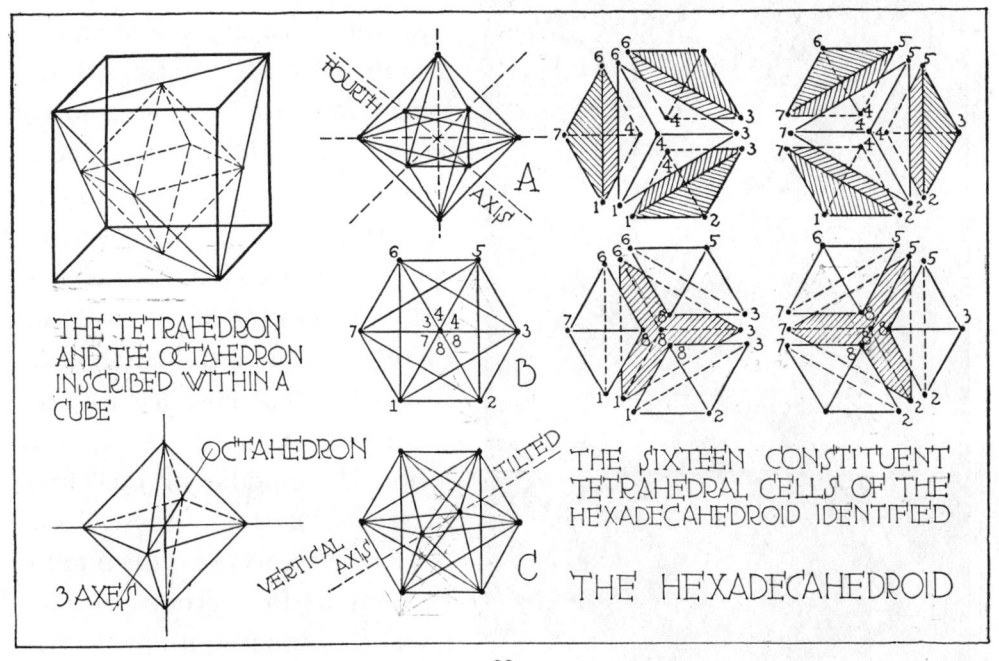

![Illustration 68: The tetrahedron and the octahedron inscribed within a cube; Octahedron 3 axes; The hexadecahedroid with fourth axis, vertical axis, tilted; The sixteen constituent tetrahedral cells of the hexadecahedroid identified.]

68

tually perpendicular and may be taken to correspond to three dimensions of space. In order to develop from the octahedron its four-dimensional correlative, the hexadecahedroid, we must provide a fourth axis at right angles to the other three. It can be only *represented;* let us represent it, therefore, by an additional dotted line passing through the center of the octahedron — the fourth perpendicular. On this axis, equidistant from the center, we establish two additional vertices. Connecting these with the others by means of lines representing the edges of the tetrahedral cells, we have a diagram of a hexadecahedroid in which the number of the vertices, edges, and tetrahedral cells is found to be correct (A, Illustration 68).

If we imagine we are looking directly down at this figure along the vertical axis, its representation would change to that shown in B. But the two vertices along the axis of vision are then represented by a single point, and the far and near edges coincide, so we *tilt* the figure just a little, and its aspect will then have changed to that shown in C.

All three are different diagrammatic representations of the hexadecahedroid, accurate so far as it is possible to make them, and correct as to the number of vertices, edges, faces, cells. As the reader may have some difficulty in counting and identifying these sixteen tetrahedral cells from the diagrams, let us pull the 16-hedroid apart, as it were. Using the middle of the three diagrams for this purpose, Illustration 68 shows the sixteen tetrahedrons in four groups of four each, the vertices numbered as in the parent figure, for purposes of identification. The employment of one of these "nests" of tetrahedrons as a motif for ornament is shown in Illustration 69.

69

The interested reader may pursue this same method with regard to the pentahedroid and the hypercube, developing the diagrams first, and then dissecting them. Entirely aside from the uses of these figures as aids to the designing of ornament, such exercises as this give glimpses, open up vistas, into the wonderland of the fourth dimension, while as a mental gymnastic and means of developing the imagination, they are unexcelled.

The diagrammatic representation of the more complicated regular polyhedroids I shall not here attempt, lest I go counter to the true spirit and purpose of this book, which is intended to be provocative, stimulative, suggestive, with only so much of chapter and verse from the bible of mathematics as to point my moral and adorn my tale — to assure the reader that he is on safe though vertiginous ground.

SINBAD PUSHES ASUNDER THE TESSERACT CUBES TRYING TO FIND THE FOURTH DIMENSION

SINBAD DISCOVERS THE SPECTRAL COLORS LATENT IN THE LIGHT OF THE SUN

IX
COLOR

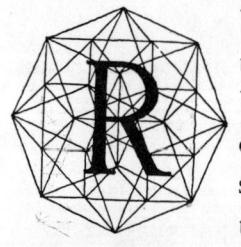

RUSKIN was right when he said that anyone could learn to draw — he was himself an admirable draughtsman — but only those who were to the manner born could become colorists. For the color sense, like the musical sense, appears to be a *gift*, and though amenable to training and development in everyone, it is so only within limits which the born colorist — like the born composer in the field of music — will easily overpass.

No book purporting to deal, like this one, with the elements of decorative design as applied particularly to architecture, can omit some discussion of color, for polychromy is entering into architecture more and more, but color cannot be *taught*, effectively — least of all from books. That is to say, no amount of instruction will make a person a *good* colorist; the most that it can do is to prevent him from being a bad one. All that I shall attempt to do, therefore, is to present a few fundamental facts and ideas which, like a knowledge of dynamic symmetry, should be part of the equipment of every designer. Everything beyond this one must learn by actual experimentation — if one can and as one can.

The first thing is to become aware of the inevitable bisection of the color spectrum into cold colors and warm — electric and thermal. Roughly, the colors of higher vibration — from green to violet — belong to the first category, and those of lower vibration — from red to green — to the second. But any color, from either segment, may itself be warm or cold to the contrasted aspect of itself. That is to say, there can be a cold violet and a warm violet; a cold (greenish) yellow and a warm — there can even be a cold red relatively to another red. Some of the most satisfactory color combinations consist of the cold and warm of a single color, with just enough of the complementary to make them "live more abundantly."

The next thing is to become aware of complementaries. The complementary of a color may be compared to the reciprocal of a number; for just as in mathematics a reciprocal is a function or expression so related to another that their product is unity, the complementary of any given color is such another color from the opposite part of the spectrum that, when combined with it, cancels it, so to speak; yielding, in pigment, neutral grey; in light, white.

Because the secret of color harmony and color brilliance dwells in nothing so much as in the right application of the law of complementaries, the student should make it his first business to know what colors are complementary to each other. He finds this out most amusingly — as one finds out lovers — by bringing them together and observing how they act and react. For complementaries *are* lovers, longing for union, shining brightest when in juxtaposition, supplementing and completing each other. Complementary colors should be learned and committed to memory, just as a musician recognizes and remembers consonant musical tones. This can be done in several different ways; one is by the manipulation of pigments; another and a better, by experimenting with colored light. One learns by these means, for example, that the color of the shadow of an object — on white — will always be the complementary of the color of the light which casts the shadow. But lacking the necessary paraphernalia for this order of experimentation, there is another which is simplicity itself, already described by me in "Light as a Language" in *Old Lamps for New*:

Assemble a number of brightly tinted squares of paper or silk of different colors — including the primaries — and in a strong natural light lay them, one after another, in the middle of a sheet of white paper, gazing at each one fixedly until the eye experiences retinal fatigue. After a time a fringe or nimbus of the complementary color will begin to appear around the edge of the colored bit, and if this then be removed quickly, the place it occupied will seem to be suffused by the complementary, which will slowly grow paler and finally disappear. The combinations discovered in this way should be noted and memorized, and the experiments repeated until one can tell beforehand, in any given case, what color will appear. The preconceived mental image and the perceived optical image should then be compared and the former corrected by the latter.

Another exercise to the same end is the manipulation of colored gelatines or bits of stained glass against the light, superimposing one over another and noting the colors which result from these combinations. When that result is a perfectly neutral grey, the two colors which produced it are complementaries. Van Deering Perrine, the landscape-painter — a great colorist — used to amuse himself after this fashion with a toy of his own devising. It consisted of two cylindrical pasteboard containers, one within the other, in the sides of which he had cut round holes, similarly located and spaced. These holes, four in each cylinder, he had then covered with silk dyed red, blue, green, and yellow. Into the center of this contraption he dropped a small electric light, and by turning the outer container about he brought the different colors opposite one another, thus forming others. He used to sit for hours in the dark with this instrument in his hands, as charmed by the beauty of his color-music as a musician at the keyboard of an organ.

Having used the word "color-music," this is perhaps the place to say a little something on the much-discussed analogy between color and sound — the rainbow hues and the musical scale. Within limits clear and inescapable, this analogy is true only in a limited way and up to a certain point: if pressed too far it is full of pitfalls for the artist. It provides an excellent approach, however, to the study of color: of little use to the master, it is of service to the neophyte because by means of it he may learn about color in an orderly way.

The solar spectrum, proceeding by an infinite number of gradations from red at one end and violet at the other, may be compared to the

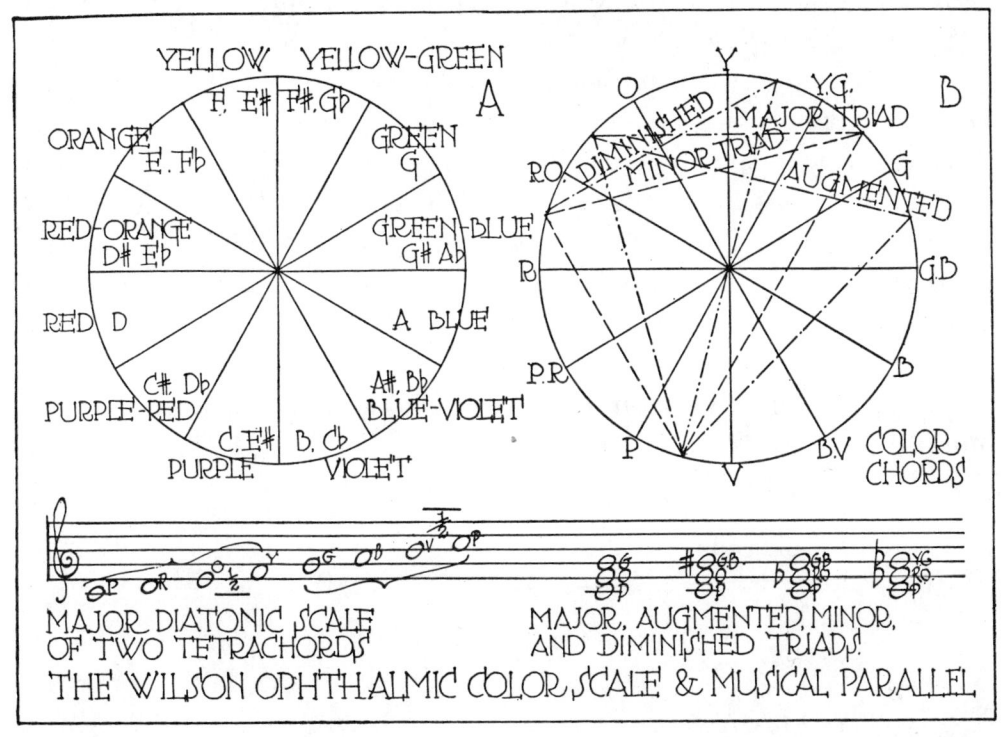

THE WILSON OPHTHALMIC COLOR SCALE & MUSICAL PARALLEL

sound of a siren which begins on one note and ascends to its octave. The color-band and this sound are equally capable of being artificially subdivided. The so-called chromatic scale in music represents a twelvefold subdivision of the sound-octave, and if the color-octave be similarly dealt with, it is clear that there would be a color to correspond with every note of the chromatic scale. In this splitting-up of the spectrum, however, an *equal* subdivision cannot be adhered to — the color-band must be more or less arbitrarily dealt with. By reason of this fact (among others) the various color-scales which have been suggested differ in detail from one another, though most of them make red correspond to the tonic, or middle C, and the deviations from one another of the other color " notes " do not as a rule amount to more than what in music would be a semitone.

Of these color scales — Rimington's, Taylor's, and others — the so-called " ophthalmic color scale " developed by Mr. Louis Wilson, is the most useful, since it embraces a greater range of purples, a color indispensable to the artist. Mr. Wilson makes " royal purple " — which is a deep sanguine, or blood-color, not a violet — the tonic of his scale (although of course, as in music, every color is the tonic of a scale of its own). He omits orange-yellow and violet-purple from his twelvefold subdivision, which makes his scale correspond more exactly with the major diatonic scale of two tetrachords, in which there is a difference of only a semitone between the next to the last note (E and F, and B and C, in the scale of C major). The scale has also the great merit that when its twelve colors are arranged in the form of a circle, the complementaries occupy positions exactly or very nearly opposite to each other as will be seen by reference to Illustation 70. Here follows Wilson's scale with its musical correlatives:

Purple	C, B#
Purple-red	C#, D♭
Red	D
Red-orange	D#, E♭
Orange	E, F♭
Yellow	F, E#
Yellow-green	F#, G♭
Green	G
Green-blue	G#, A♭
Blue	A
Blue-violet	A#, B♭
Violet	B, C♭

It is evident that by the use of this scale some sort of translation of musical chords — and indeed of entire compositions — into their color correlatives is rendered possible. The thing has been done — I have done it myself — and the results are interesting and instructive; they are also beautiful, for colored light is seldom unbeautiful, but not more so than could be arrived at by means more direct. For the beauty of any given color combination depends almost entirely upon the right adjustment of relative *areas* and relative *values,* things unrelated to music, to the determination of which therefore the musical parallel can give no help. In color-translation musical consonances are often found to be less satisfactory than dissonances, and there are color combinations of extraordinary beauty of which a correlative musical expression gives no hint — like a passage from warm to cold of a given color together with its complementary (purple, purple-red, red, red-orange, orange, and green-blue, for example) ; in music all this would amount to would be a chromatic run of five notes and the fourth of the middle one of them.

As a matter of fact there are *no* ugly color combinations if they are dealt with in a manner which gives due regard to areas and values. Modern music appears to be built on the same assumption with regard to sound — that all is relative. Be that as it may, the law of complementaries is a better guide and safeguard (in so far as there *is* any guide and safeguard other than an intuitive color sense) than any labored translation of musical chords into color chords. Moreover, an intelligent application of the law of complementaries leads to much the same results but in a more direct way. For example, a color triad based on the law of complementaries would consist in " splitting " a given color and combining these two halves with its complementary (purple, orange, and green-blue, or yellow-green, blue-violet, and red) . In our color-wheel these would define an equilateral triangle, and would correspond in music to an augmented triad. Major, minor, and diminished triads, picked out on the color-wheel in this way, also define triangles the vertices of which meet the " rim " never less than three " spokes " apart. Knowing this fact, should one choose to depend upon a mechanical method for obtaining harmonious color combinations, this system of triangulation is easier and more direct than the translation of musical chords into color chords by means of the musical analogy. Experimentation along these lines is helpful and educative, but it should always be remembered that the law of complementaries is the master-key to the color mystery in so far as there is any key at all. It is one, however, which gives access only to the anteroom of that enchanted castle, for with the three variables of hue, area, and intensity only the born colorist can successfully deal.

Mr. Fritz Trautmann, who starts from the vantage ground of being a born colorist, has for a number of years been studying and experimenting along original lines. The results of his researches he has not formulated as yet, but he has been gracious enough to permit me to transcribe part of a letter containing the core of his theory, from the application of which, in both painting and teaching, he has achieved remarkable results:

The most subtle and penetrating vibrations coming to us from the sun — the so-called ultra-violet ray — is the one that most definitely affects the skin, as is evidenced by sun-tan; and as the eye is the part of the skin most sensitively adapted or tuned to the sun's rays, it would seem that this most sensitive spot should make a natural — or normal — response to violet. We know that when any material is so constituted in its crystalline structure that it absorbs light of a given color, that material takes on an external aspect of all the rest of the light that is turned back — in other words, the complement. Now it is an interesting fact, and I think a significant one, that the physiologists have discovered that the pigmentation of that most sensitive spot on the retina is yellow, and they call it the yellow spot.

This is the underlying basis of my theory: The sun is the affector, the eye is the receptor. All phenomenal aspects occur between the two. It requires both affector and receptor for the conception of white light. So for us who live under the sun, the violet-yellow axis becomes the personal axis or beginning place for all color sensation. I have never had a group of students disagree about the location of these poles on the color-wheel or fail to isolate them from the other hues. Once they have made that judgment, the explanation of color action becomes simple: All the rest of it is a sort of emotional tremor imparted to the personal axis. I drive two tacks in a screen, one some distance above the other, and over these I stretch a rubber band. The top tack is yellow — the light of the eye: bright, luminous, revealing. The bottom tack is violet — helios, the sun — profound, deep, penetrating. If I grasp one half of the band — midway between the tacks or not — and stretch it out to the right, the personal axis is distorted or deflected, with the maximum of deflection occurring at the point where my finger happens to be. If I pull the band out to the left, the axis is again disturbed, but the extreme point of the disturbance is exactly opposite in nature and complementary to the one on the right. I ask the class to identify these extremes on the color wheel, and I give appropriate names to designate their emotional appeal. Here, again, I have never had a group fail to agree on their location, even to a surprising degree of precision, and there is never any doubt about their feeling that one side is hot and the other cold. When it comes to color notation I find that there is usually some difference of opinion as to what these extreme places should be called. Almost everyone will agree on *red* as the name of the hot extreme, but *blue* is a name so long associated with a color containing a large dose of violet that many object to it as applied to the cold extreme. On the other hand, they also reject the term *blue-green* because the green part of the term implies a content of yellow, and they are quick to discern that the disturbance of the personal axis equally affects both poles and that no point can be considered extreme so long as it contains an element of either yellow or violet. Strange to say, however, the terms *redness* and *blueness* seem to satisfy the majority of any group, so I let it go at that and impress upon them that the name is really of little importance so long as they are sure of the quality.

This should be enough to give you the kernel of my whole idea. All of the intervening colors between these four critical points are considered as the two primary personal poles (yellow and violet), merely being cooled or warmed to succeeding degrees. White and black to me are neutrals, always secondary effects, the result of complementaries acting together — interacting. Dodge McKnight paints the whitest of snow with red and blue pigment. He could as well do it with yellow and violet or any other pair, depending on the time of day — the mood.

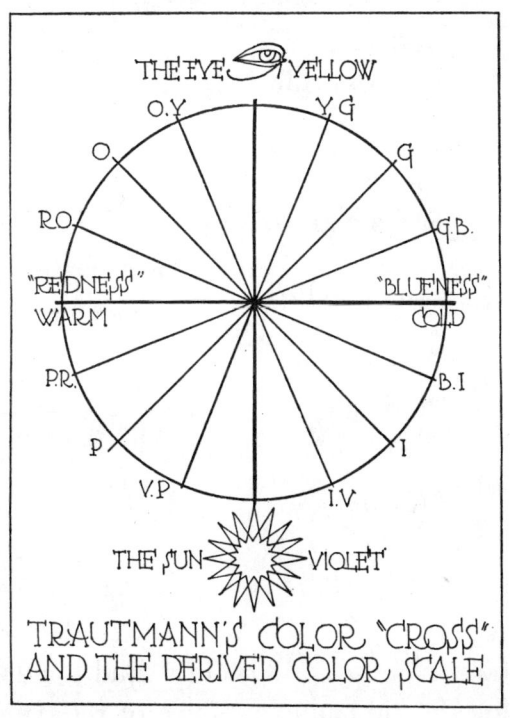

71

This seems to me a better approach to the subject of color than by way of the musical parallel, although the conclusions and results may prove to be identical. A graphic expression of Mr. Trautmann's idea would consist of a cross of which the vertical axis would have yellow at the top and violet at the bottom, and the horizontal axis " redness " at the left and " blueness " at the right (Illustration 70). Comparing this with the Wilson color-wheel, it will be seen that these colors occupy the same relative position, and that there is no essential contradiction between them. In Trautmann's cross the intermediate spaces between his four " primaries " may be bisected, yielding the " secondaries " * orange, green, indigo, and purple, a color scale of eight notes; or trisected, yielding a scale of twelve, in all essentials like the Wilson scale. If a more minute subdivision be required, the total may be increased to sixteen, in which case it would read as follows:

    Violet
    Violet-purple
    Purple
    Purple-red
    Red
    Red-orange
    Orange
    Orange-yellow
    Yellow
    Yellow-green
    Green
    Green-blue
    Blue
    Blue-indigo
    Indigo
    Indigo-violet

It would be well for the student of color to use this scale, which is both adequate and orderly; and to adopt also this terminology, abandoning the ridiculous practice of referring to colors by those arbitrary and meaningless names by which they are currently known. But in so doing one should keep clearly and constantly in mind what I have said about it, and particularly the " color cross " — as a mariner keeps in mind the cardinal points of the compass.

    The color-world is *par excellence* a world of relativity: colors alter

---

* Trautmann says, "I don't like the term 'secondaries' as applied to any pure phase of the spectrum. You see, I have only one primary action — the personal axis and its extremes of amplitude. Secondaries seem to me to be the result of damping or interference."

COLOR

their appearance in changed relations and proportions and under different conditions of atmosphere and illumination. A color may be made to appear warm or cold, to advance or to retreat, by an alteration of adjacent colors, and it in turn affects them. In this, more than in any other department of the fine arts, each must work out his own salvation with relatively little outside aid. Belonging as it does to the domain of feeling rather than of thinking, the intuition rather than the reason should be one's guide. Over and above what I have already said, perhaps the only further instruction which can be given is summarized in the words: *observe, reflect, feel, and experiment.*

SINBAD OBSERVING AND STUDYING COLOR AND LIGHT

DATE DUE			
DEC 14 84			
30 505 JOSTEN'S			